The Invisib]

Selected Poems

David Morley's poetry has won numerous awards and prizes. An ecologist and naturalist by background, David is also known for his pioneering ecological poetry installations within natural landscapes and the creation of 'slow poetry' sculptures and I-Cast poetry films. He writes essays, criticism and reviews for the *Guardian* and *Poetry Review*. A leading international advocate of creative writing both inside and outside the academy, David is the author of *The Cambridge Introduction to Creative Writing* (2007) and co-editor of *The Cambridge Companion to Creative Writing* (2012). He currently teaches at the University of Warwick where he is Professor of Writing.

Also by David Morley from Carcanet Press

Scientific Papers
The Invisible Kings
Enchantment
The Gypsy and the Poet

DAVID MORLEY

The Invisible Gift
Selected Poems

CARCANET

First published in Great Britain in 2015 by
Carcanet Press Limited
Alliance House
Cross Street
Manchester M2 7AQ

www.carcanet.co.uk

ISBN 978 1 84777 206 0

The publisher acknowledges financial assistance from Arts Council England

Typeset by XL Publishing Services, Exmouth
Printed and bound in England by SRP Ltd, Exeter

Contents

III

IV

Epilogue

Prologue

Hedgehurst

So out stepped this young man – half hedgehog and half human being. And the king stood and looked: he'd never seen a creature like this in all his days.

He said, 'What type of being are you that could do all this? Have you anyone to help you?'

'No,' said the hedgehurst, 'I need help from no-one.'

'You mean to tell me,' says the king, 'that you built this place by yourself and you cut all these trees, built all these things and made this place like this?' It was the most beautiful place the king had ever seen.

'I have,' said the hedgehurst, 'I've done all this myself. But anyway, getting back to you: what is it you want of me, for I am king of this and this is my kingdom.'

'I want nothing from you', says the king. 'But I am amazed! Tell me, what are you?'

He said, 'I am a hedgehurst.'

– Duncan Williamson, *Fireside Tales of the Traveller Children*

I am Hedgehurst. I, snow-
slumbering, the loaf of my body
ovened in a bole beneath
a flame-leafed sycamore,
uncurl from my coiled hole.
Whose is this scorned skin?
What weather rouses me
to lag my limbs with lichen,
to fold fresh thatch around me?
I roll, I loll in fallen leaves.
They melt me asleep; I
blunder through dream,
weaving that way then this,
from Februaries of thawing
to nodding November.
My mind measures out claw points,

paw prints but snarls me into a ball.
A jury of jays jabs me, scolds me.
Why are you dozing here? they jabber.
What, what is, what is your story?

Born blunt, born blind, I pawed
the mist of my mother,
sensed her shawl around
me like leaf-dry shelter.
Her love, a raw rend across
her womb; she wore my birth
along her thighs in rips, in wounds.
Childless, she had chided
my father in tears, in years,
until overheard by a wider world –
in the sleight of a stranger who
held a hedgehog on her palm,
who smiled her spell through
their walls. Worlds were unspun.
I nosed through that cottage
for six years, eye-high to its locks.
Outside, my father's axe lit
lightning from the oak's flint barks.
When I found my feet
I floundered forwards on all fours.

My father flared and fumed as
I fumbled with gravities.
I lapped spilled milk while he
watched me, as wary as a hare.
My bed was strewn stale straw.
I lay still on my spines'
springs, napping on my nails.
My father's weasel whine
seeped and stole through
my rough wall each drab night.
My mother's muteness was enough
to shut me into some bright

burial ground of myself, to grind
her halved child into ground.
I was the space between an axe-edge
and the oak's white wound.
I was seven in nothing but age
when I left home with no word.
I wound my way through the walls
of their world and into this wood.

The tines of my pelt, draggling,
made me stronger as I went;
and, when I made camp,
found myself no stranger
to that wood's world. I called
my name into the night. The trees
shushed me, then answered
with caterpillars baited on threads.
I called again. Moths moored
in bark-fissures flickered out,
fluttered towards me as I spoke
as though my voice was alight.
Pipistrelles unfurled through firs.
Fireflies bloomed and doused.
I called until dawn into the next
dawn. I spun and unspun their names
with my name. When I had worlded
the woods with these creatures
I lounged on my spines.
I then called out the birds.

Clamorous as alphabets in a cloud,
starlings strew down. They settled
like a harvest in the highest
trees and sang, drizzling.
Then came magicians, green
woodpeckers, the greenest men.
They were circling laughter. They
were soft rolls on the oak's drum.

Ceremonially stabbing his prey
on haw, sloe, dog-rose,
a shrike shrieked down to feast,
his larder stiff on thorns.
Woodpigeons unwarped their wings,
clapping through larch canopies.
Wrens buzzed from bushes. Tree-
creepers moused up yew-
towers. Rolled bodily from a nest
a solitary cuckoo came
closer than comfort, bearing
her unchilding charm.

Arcing down the air's stair silently,
those emblems – snowy owls
bowed whitely then blinked.
In the brimming underworld below
their bowing branches, ptarmigans
moved, still smooth with snow.
I kept my call up – the starlings
now imitating – so I swerved it,
narrowed it, arrowed my voice
down the bolt-holes of hedgerows,
calling up the fields and the further
afields of floodplain, lake, river.
A tarn's surface flickered with the ore
of rudd, orfe and roach.
Dace, carp, and loach spun
on their rudders to the fly of my call.
I viewed the arc of my kingdom:
a rainbow righting itself above water,
its likeness mirrored and ringed
under and above the surface of all things.

I latticed hedges in high-tension
about the wood's borders,
their branches barred, all twigs
cats-cradled. No low doors for badgers.

No runnels for runaways. Even roots
rammed deeper. Those windows
between leaf and leaf I made
shatter-proof with web and web, spiders
garrisoning them like a million eyes
in a wall. For twenty years I had peace
when a door unlatched where no door
was, its hasps hidden in a space
of a second guess. Striding in circles
of his own dream, a hunting king
came upon my clearing while I crafted;
needling me for directions, marvelling
at my work. I needed help from no-one,
so returned that king to his kind,
he, gifting his word that the first thing he saw
within the world elsewhere would be mine.

I had kenned from my wrens
how to cave-mine my call,
to speak through soil, make
speech slither through a hill,
and I learned from my bats
and owls how to hear it all back,
the echo resounding slow
in the swirl and swoon of a beck,
given tongue as it trickles from
rock-pool to spill murmurs
along a lake-bed, passed through
caddis-fly to bloodworm to fish
before the catch is ospreyed
up from the water and sprayed
back through the nets in my ear.
In this way I overheard
the worlds outside my wood:
how the king had come home,
how his daughter, his dearest child,
had been the first to greet him.

But no word reached me. I let
the seasons sing themselves slow.
I let the winds wind through
on their migrations. I lay
my ear to the lake and listened.
Silence and then ice. Jays
mocked me to life in March.
I rose and called twice
for what it would take –
I called all my creatures.
I could make war with water,
by damming ducts, flash-floods,
by underwhelming wells but I
could not take a field with fish.
I had noise enough to light out
for territory – snipe's throb, woodpecker's
drum, stork's clack, heron's bill-clap,
and at dawn, the lapwing's thrum.
The birds went before me, and my army,
the earth's creatures, they followed me.

Fat rain soaks an unwringable soil.
The sun's hand fumbles at a rag
of earth. It can do nothing with it
but shape steam or ice. The slog
of roots as they ply through rock,
murk, moisture – this was my work
that half-day. When rain runs
over rain, when deep roots are delved,
high banks breached, the araucaria's
canopy's reefed, leaf-land on a lake,
drench-drowned, its green throat
gasping; so it was when we
showed up at that king's fences
and forts; he, done over in a
heartbeat, his whole kingdom
drowned by hoof-beats, antlers
clattering in his pallid palace;

and his people, his, peering
from their portholes, from
prison ships of their tenements.

Leaves allow answers to a season:
when to give way, when to hold
hard. I had these humans
in the hands of my branches.
I held them up to the Spring:
showed them the month's doors
opening on each other, those
rain-crafted courtyards of a year;
offered them the openings
of a fern, the currencies
of those smote-eyed seeds;
gave them the conditions
written in grass-blades
as a wind wicks through them;
read softly the rules
of the rain as it retreated
to its ravines and rivers;
and when this was done
the king's daughter came to me
without question or hesitation.

In the broken and in the woken
dreams of the king's people
I moved to teach the tongues
torn from them: my creatures' calls.
In the palace hall, the court spoke
at me on their stilts of speech;
I scythed those sticks: tottering
tongues stammered and spilled.
In the city I was the space
between a shrike's spike and prey.
I was a holly bush among them.
Carnivalled in star-lit nails
I nightwalked the city. Will

to will, my wife met me,
while the silk king sulked.
For its wands of low light
to wane through the windows
to douse my blood, to slow me,
to slow me so and so clench me
that coward king waited on winter.

My beasts were busy unweaving
and reweaving the city: woodwasps
worked the wrecked timbers
of the tenements, ravens
refreshed the roofs. Snipe,
scaup and scoter settled
at reservoirs, sweetened inrunning
rivers, drilled then dredged
the silts and sands. Crossbills
and finches fossicked field-seed;
horses hauled those harvests home.
I foddered my creatures by starlight
steeling my skin against the moon's
zero. My hearth held some secrecy
of spring: to win through winter
I would need that fire's hand.
Each night I knelt nearer its blaze.
I strained with my spines. I stripped
myself clear of my cladding, then
made my way numb beneath the moon.

Three nights with my nerves
on knives; three nights clad
in the cold's clay; my hearth,
pelt and wife waiting for me at dawn.
I was almost blunt and blind,
my mother's mist rising
as I yanked fodder to the stalls
calling creature to creature.
On the third midnight I plucked

then placed my pelt. My wife
watched from our bed then
waving once, wondered to sleep.
I staggered through a sheer snow
of stars. I made everyone safe.
I smelled before I saw my broad
skin broiling where the king
had stoked it high on a bonfire.
And then the king came to me,
soldiers before him, bright buckets
jagged and acid with ice-water.

The water's wile, the wound of it,
it winded my mind; its ice spermed
through my veins, hatched in my heart.
Breath blew from me and I fell
into a glacier of my blood. I saw
the king handed my father's axe;
my wife running from her room,
out from dream; and then
his daughter flying at him, bearing
down on a boar, her white
wrists writhing. All this. I saw all this
before a wind flew back through me
and I whispered my wife's name.
The stars shushed me, then
answered me with caterpillars
baited on threads. I called her again.
Moths stirred in bark-fissures.
They flickered out, fluttered
towards us as I spoke her name,
as though my voice was a light.

Overheard by a wider world
I called the kennings of the people: spun
and unspun their names, emparadising them,
shaping, smiling a spell through their walls –

Adder and Anemone   Badger and Bear
Corncrake and Curlew   Deer and Dragonfly
Earwig and Elver   Fox and Firecrest
Grebe Grasshopper   Hoverfly Hare
Ibis and Iguana   Jackdaw and Jay
Kittiwake Kingfisher   Lapwing Lacewing
Mole and Merganser   Nuthatch and Nightjar
Oriole and Otter   Pike and Plover
Quail Rabbit Ruff   Smew Salamander
Twite and Turnstone   Urchin and Viper
Wryneck Wheatear   Yaffle and Zander

worlding the king's people with the coats
and calls of these creatures, weaving
halls and walls into our woods
and when this was done
their world was mine.

Ramsons whiten into life, slow-
slumbering through the thaw.
After spring showers, my halved
children will tread paths sprung
and sewn from their scent alone.
I wake half-dreaming. For seconds
I do not know myself. What hands
are these that are lacerable
but sprung with spines?
What weather rouses me,
unclenches my limbs from frost?
Where is my second skin?
It is winter gone.   It is worlds unspun.
I judder awake as jays bounce
and strut about my body.
I rise, I shout, and they scatter.
They jump screaming into the sky.
It is time to call everything to life
for I am king of this and this is my kingdom.

Who am I?   I am Hedgehurst.

I

The Site

after Mandelshtam

Why am I trailing you,
now through a pinewood, now
through the words I write,
going nowhere fast?

There's a Gypsy encampment on the steppes,
newly moved in – sharp fires gone
by morning; the stamped ash
surrenders no clue or forwarding address.

I am in the pinewoods, trailing you.
There you were, like memory, a shackle.
Cling to me, you said.

Voronezh, January 1937

Clearing a Name

Spindrift across Stalmine, a place you won't know.
Reedbeds, gyp sites; flat Lancashire's Orinoco.

I watch a mistle-thrush on a blown telegraph wire,
leave my car by the dead elm above the river.

The camp is two caravans. The police have just left.
Two blue-tacked Court Orders this wind can't shift

or the rain read. A girl squatting with a carburettor
on her bare knees. Another, older, in a deck-chair

spoons Pot Noodle. Their dad with his pride, no joy,
wrestles over the yawning bonnet of a lorry.

Mam is out, knocking Blackpool's door
with her basket of tack, toddler dressed-down with care

for the rending detail: no shoes. I watch
the father unbend, fumble at the fire, splice a match

from a stray half-wicker, then I come down.
He lets a welcome wait in another time,

twists a roll-up, nods OK to his staring daughters.
Eyes me like fresh scrap fenced from a dealer,

half-sorted, half-known. Yes; he knew our family
'more for what they were' – Hop-girls, Iron-boys –

'but they married out, and there's the end of it.
Your muck's paid no muck of ours a visit.'

A thin smile: 'Except your dad,
he came with the nose of Concorde

on worksheets reeking of grease and swarfega,
bleating "an inch is now a bloody centimetre".

What's up with your schools? I'd say. Him – "This *is* school."
We squinnied blueprints as if they were braille.

Taught ourselves ground-up. A small conversion.
If your muck had stayed in family, if your gran

hadn't gone nosing *gaujo* like they were the end-all.
Now you've had your end, fair do's. Get off pal,

you're not burnt up on fags or dodgy work.'

The ends, we want; the means are half the work:

something in his grip, under my sleeve like veins,
where hands lock together, become the same,

'Arctic on Antarctica'... *I need background.*
The uncle on my mother's side. 'Pulled from a pond.

The police were out for a man. Any taig or gyp.
Guns broke for a chicken-shoot. They found him face-up

and it fitted. They shot shite in a barrel.'
That B-road where Lancashire discharges its spoil.

Split mattresses. Paint tins. Grim stuff in carriers.
The sign No Dumping No Travellers.

I make my way back to the car, running
the hard keys from hand to hand then, turning,

pocket them. I do not move. It is not smart to show
(that plain car by the woods) how and where you go.

One uncle of mine went swimming. His name is snow,
or thaw, or mud. And you wouldn't know.

Moonlighter

He might be my brother for all he is gyp.
His is not the time for pullovers and combs;
his plum shirt is Blackpool, very Blackpool.
I have watched his van for hours, from Marton Estate
to this traveller site; a mole in mole's clothing.
He will scrabble through the mud of everything:
the nuts and nuggets of marriage, a bolt of a ring,
weights of children, slack pulleys of police.
Burglar by night, a rain-soaked genius
of the jerry-built coastal pre-fab,
he stacks his van with valuables:
a deadman, a handspike, a parbuckle.
Lightning moves its show across the camp.

Three

I am trying to behave but my father
has a fist crammed with kitchen knives
like a brilliant new hand, and the rest
of us in the house are suddenly not alive.
One of us is guilty of the crime of two biscuits.
One of us has taken biscuits without permission
so all are condemned and have earned his lesson
which is to cower in the bedroom's corner
without cover while he slices our arteries open
in the air between us. His house is his abattoir.
His home is lit with hooks and steel hands.
We are not alive as he bars the bedroom door.

The morning is ordinary because I am three.
My brother unwinds a lace from his shoe.
He works its little rope across the hearth

until it makes a dripping strip of light and flame
that he slips slowly on the back of my hand.
I am trying to behave as though this never happened,
keeping my scorched hand below the tablecloth
while my father, sick with guilt, serves us soup.
My brother knows I can soak up his secrets.
My left fingers misbehave and my father
forces the hand. Seared open. Veal of vein.
My brother at this time is being flung into a wall
and all I am thinking is that I do not like oxtail.

I do not like the blood thirst of what I can hear
through the floor of my bedroom as my father
flies off his handle again, but this is a real handle
that he's handling as a weapon, and the sitting room
is being smashed and smashed and smashed to death.
Better the mirrors, I think, than my mother.
But he's upstairs by now, kicking his way up
and dread is draining through that black wall
but the wall doesn't shelter, not when there's a door
to be hurled off its hinges like it was never there,
him yanking me by my cock to his yelling height
before dropping me down a well in that dark room.
His face swells to fill the door as he finds his range.

Σ

Our family eats the funeral sandwiches: pink paste and white bread.
My saucy Scouse uncles pinch at their bits of tobacco.
They fall, clawing at fake heart attacks each time I come up to them.

We are in the kitchen of my dead grandmother's maisonette.
Her sisters squawk about compensation, weather, and the Third Eye.
One of my aunts goes spare: 'What's dead is dead.
We're small people. We can't take on the whole bloody NHS.'

The internal pressure burst the capillaries beneath my gran's eye
diagonally, like a whip might, opening her hale cheekbone up.
Sigma is the shape carved on that seventy-year-old face
where the care-worker screwed his fist around her nose to smash it.

Wasp

They found you cold, fists jammed on each other,
Arctic on Antarctica. And between them,
paper, scrawl: a crumpled note signed and sealed.
To release it meant prising a wrist,
cheating the knot of rigor mortis.
Then a policeman picked it with a jemmy…

Just once, this once, make sense of me?
Her words, questing, tightened their wire
across my chest. The car where they found you,
shut windows weeping with monoxide,
was hauled away; sold off to strangers
at a cut price they never fathomed.

Lies. All of it… a first, final readership,
hostaged to your death, in a coroner's office.
You should have shared. You didn't.
All this time… all that time, *you knew.*
Your parents bunched, stark as witnesses;
made for the door. You'd cut the ice.

Solstitial visitor, always the wasp
in your quick-fire combing along my shelves.
Were those books your pollen?
or the excuse for returning them
unread, spurning discussion
with a thrumming whisper, *bed?*
All reasons for talk squandered, unheard.
Only fear of love unsheathed your sting.

Ice. Our first winter: a glassy hive.
Honey in jars – bottles, sidelong,
whispered KILNER, KILN… KIL…
I dipped a spoon in the first of the year,
tugging the surface to a muscle of lava;
slipped it, neat, in your bowl of coffee.
Half-love, your love's language:
you stirred its black spiral.

Snow. December; castanets of hail;
holly we brought in snared with hooks.
Taps betrayed us, a clanking mutiny
bursting a wall. We boiled snow:
snow on snow. Our windows, portholed
on a white atlantic, silently froze.
Bed, with the fire's dying collusion,
gave up its gift as we crammed for warmth.

Leaving unspoken what the doctor told you,
the clack of your step said: *Don't, don't,
don't…* I cut to the kitchen, jabbing
a kettle's thick, cool waist for coffee.
London in March. A second opinion
grudged the first. *Anything to be done?*
Nothing between us the train couldn't say,
hammering northward: *too late too late.*

Not now: your touchy, embattled cry
as I steered you from silence, hoping you'd walk
a little of the way. 'The woods perhaps?
a tree-creeper's nested.' But: *No – you
go.* I'd veer out, make eighty yards
before I stopped, stranded with wonder:
your seeping, last hours (minute by minute)
creeping like a bird on shrivelled bark.

That silence. I tried it.
An anchor scudding the sea-floor,
you were snared on a weightless sand;
for days you couldn't move or speak.
Then, a false spring:
you asked for food; for your bed
to be placed in the hall-way
as though you'd fledge.

Your silence was fear, furled like a sting.
Your dad called by to run you to hospital.
Wants me to go and get it over!
You swayed to the car where your father
sat smoking. *Cunt – I'll die
where I like*
slamming to the bedroom,
snatching your things.

They found you cold, the car's drained engine
ticking to zero; you, flexed over yourself,
catapulted to that final wish: an Arctic quiet;
the sealight torching your eye like a mirror…
I came home to cupboards – their after-life, memory;
your clothes strewn-about, burgled from wardrobes.
And the garden: its hive, a Vesuvius of larvae,
fresh tenants of this frozen site.

The Goodnight

An owl unfolds across the bed:
its eyes, hungover can see the dead;
the swerving and the narrow hours
are no longer mine, no longer yours:
perfect ships of life and work
butt each other in the dark.

While adulterers in their box-rooms stuff
straw into their whinnying love,
and swimmers-out-of-sight clear
the deep-water and the disappear,
dreamers in their tents will know
that snow will light the night for now.

Light we taught to obey our touch
is surrendered to the switch.
The asthma of our deaths goes deep.
We are not alive in sleep:
the panic of my child at night
is the world's unbearable flight.

Mathematics of Light

The wavelengths of daylight
register on bright equipment:

flutterings across a spectrum
from infra-red to ultraviolet.

Discover me at an ice age,
at a midnight of colour,

in a place where rainbows
unbind themselves completely.

But you stand in the noon.
Shadows are inventing themselves

over your quickening retina;
the day moves on to shade

when spires are like pen-strokes
in the heat haze… It's

like Newton's gold trances
as he skimmed slates on the sea,

like Einstein's chatter over tea,
borealis, wispy cigarettes. It's

down to the human to live it, take
it in. Keep my sunlight warm for me.

Oceanography

i

Apart from the sea we have the weather
in common, but the morning moves on
like a dunlin, precarious, stilt-walking
on her own reflection. A steamer's vapour
has collapsed on itself over the ocean.

Someone is dozing beneath the low planking
of the jetty. He knows that tomorrow
the mist will deepen, again it will snow,
the sky will come with something like hail.
Meanwhile, he has a worm-ridden bed
for sleep. Meanwhile, fishermen sling nets
from the rounded bay where a single sail
slows to a cloud. The nets come up empty.

ii

The grass is marram grass and the sand, sand.
These are facts that hang on everything.
Beyond the heath are meadows that send
entire crops to the big city. Everything hinges
on this; any sign of life is the weather breathing.

After the meadows and steppes, the Volga.
River, I thought I'd mislaid you like a mirror.
For days I didn't belong to your shoreline
until I drank you down, felt your sharp tongue
etch on my voice a clear voice of water.
No mention of your tide's slow censoring;
anything can happen, and everything.

The Spectra

after Mandelshtam

I have come for you and I have seen you.
It is a miracle. For once, you're going nowhere,
neither out to walk the rounds of the horizon
nor home to scribble white lines about it.

I half see you through that knife-hole in the ice,
past shivering, staring back. Have you stopped here forever,
the record of your death still spinning,
that snow death you always longed for?

It is like this, my love, where skaters
swerve beyond you, where the horizon's lightning
makes you run any place but towards it:
it is like nothing on earth.
The sun is seven pure fires
and they in turn will come for you.

Voronezh, January 1937

The Boy and the Peacock

after Mandelshtam

What's left of the morning is probably good:
milk, tea, black bread, the minutiae of exile.
   But what we are told in this ordered room
     won't please the escort or the gods.

They've given me four years to survive my name.
(The landlord calls me everything under the sun.)
   What's left of the morning is probably good
     but it doesn't please the escort or the gods.

A farmer came today, gave us oats and kale
to make good broth, to see us through the worst.
   The escort eats his fill, goes back to bed.
     (What's left of the morning is probably good.)

So, we walk to a hill where legend has it
a boy lived with a peacock. He was thought a god.
   He fed on rainbows, scarlet milk. He *was* a god.
     It pleased everyone to think so. And they survived.

Now he's wrapped underground with all he had.
His body's his own, was it also theirs?
   They'd picked him over, found he wasn't a god
     but all too human, all too dead.

What's remembered of him can't be bad.
I like the way they buried him with seeds.
   The escort shouts us back. He thinks he's god.
     What's left of the morning is probably his.

Voronezh, December 1936

Osip Mandelshtam on the Nature of Ice

i

I'd read about glaciers and I'd seen glaciers. How a stream runs
under their bellies, sluices from their lower reaches. What it fetches
up along the way: the whole sides of mountain, gripped and ground through
its kidneys. And the taste of it as water, both sweet and sullied
or tender as blown glass. Which explains how in poems I confuse
glaciers and glaziers. Which won't explain why I am becoming
both ice and glass.

ii

He's forgetting when it started but during his exile years
they never owned a mirror. The sheen on ice supplied something
of the sort. On washing day – what little they had got bashed and
rinsed in a sink in a local theatre – he'd finger out a small
ice-mirror from a puddle, walk with Nadezhda to that grimy
theatre. And they were suddenly respectable to themselves,
staring into its tiny rink. While it lasted.

iii

How to stop ice melting from contact with live hands? Or being
flashed to crystal by every movement? I learned this on placement
in the Petersburg factories: a trick used by glaziers: slip
plate-glass in silk and, between forefinger and thumb,
gently pinch the opposing ends. It gives birth to a
pressure: it tensions lines of force which are
hurtling through the mass like waves.

iv

The secret was this: with each move he made, he
made his body ride on that new born force-field. Like
carrying a child: like walking on water: vigorously,
tenderly, he strode as if he were ice.

The charm was in the looking:
I became frozen to my image. Out of earth, out of water,
I ran clutching the ice-mirror. Through forests,
through rain. But all I know is: I
would wake walking, in controlled
free-fall, diamonds
in my fist.

Two Temperatures for Snow

As if the snow itself were a country
with pleasure gardens, hotels, religion
and the word yes and the word no.

You enter its capital along the paths of slush.
Signs direct you to the City Elder. Nothing will grow
under her rule, as Signs will tell you at every corner.

But when she invites you to her Ice Festival
you will learn to love Slowfreeze and Nightflake,
her daughters by sunless adoption. Will they dance,

dance with you? Only so slowly unless they melt
at the heart from a heat of ecstasy. The parquet
is white, white. You are falling out of life.

Their images are locked in you forever.
You will carry them, bright on your lips,
even over oceans, to your own easy gardens.

One night you may wake before dawn,
walk naked to where the river thaws
in its grave. Beneath a bridge of smoothest limestone

put your ear against the ear of winter
listening for a yes, a no. Or touch
where the words enter the water.

ii

Do none of these things. Call at the office.
When someone says yes the answer is no.
File your dockets in bin bags for burning

the moment when a stranger rides up in the elevator.
Meanwhile, talk of weather or the terrible storm damage.
Avoid words like informer, auditor, police.

There are things in the wall very like ears.
Their microphones are wonderful as knots in wood.
Listen, someone can sell you at the slightest notice

with a single nod. So they will come for you
in the small hours. To snout through your past
rabid for evidence. To ask you to repeat after them,

yes, yes, yes. Through it all they will help with heat
to the arms, chest, your white lips. Then, peace,
a dream of snow, cold hands holding you,

which you love; that lift you to where water
rushes over your face. Will you dance, dance?
Only so slowly. Melting, melting.

The Excursion to the Forest

To feed the dead who would come disguised as birds

– Czesław Miłosz

There were examples,
too many, the small people said. See, they
called, how things turn on each other
and a sleeping sickness leaks through
our language, how our Gypsy symbols spelled
no clear counsel.

O, travellers: to
ride by the river was death-wished, a flit
in the woods might end in a fight.
So what of the nightjar you were
seeking. It was the wrong time to listen,
that night hunting it.

Look, learn, sweet watcher.
There was ground to be prized in pitching here,
those small people said. The Sidh held
we had choices: the fish in this
river or the hares in those woods. Those woods,
through their white feathers,

are dark spruce. Christmas
pines, snow, one starved, star-chilled, eclipsed redbreast.
Take their bird's disguise, traveller.
They have learnt thin paths to show you
their hidden way. It was strong of you to
stride out with your heart

heard, seeking counsel.
How could they counsel, they, the watching dead –
graft to you their will of stillness
when you were snared by that river,
those woods, by Red Guards returning to their
village for Christmas.

Albert Einstein in America

i

Light is flung out of the State.
  It understands us, how our place is set.
    Escape through it.

ii

Glass heart, bone-strung feather,
    the light shapes a mirage from our sweet share.
      Escape through its weather.

iii

How the birds of sorrow
    have eaten out the heart of this running light.
      Escape through tomorrow.

iv

A cloud rows air above the groves;
    it tacks in a breeze beyond cypresses.
      Escape in their clothes.

v

Escape through their dead,
    through their teeth, bones, their vivid cramped arms.
      It is time.

The Field-Note

after Mandelshtam

Warships are breaking the ice-canals
but their bows are braced
against something
which isn't real.

There's a trail of oil spidering from the hulls.
Women and sailors stare
from the pier
where the water

booms from fantastic pumps. It says:
They wait here forever because they were never here.
The wind goes on waxing
a seagull's moustache of offal.

Voronezh, December 1936

The Aftermath

after Mandelshtam

'The dawn-trees float their dark coral
as though a sea had left them standing:
        they testify to the visible
        temerity of creation.'

'Then who has been here before us?
Who wrote us in the mist? painted our
        images into morning, as though
        we owned the faces of children?'

'It isn't always winter here:
the small fields are shaping themselves
        through the thaw. I would count on so much'.
        But the trees are a dark coral.

Voronezh, February 1937

The New Life

after Mandelshtam: after Dante

i

As with autumn, so with spring,
both tedious leave taking,

ice chinking in the gutters,
the river's ridiculous swagger.

We moved like that once,
our minds thawing with bottle after bottle.

I would sing like Dante, exhausted
by the night before, the night to come.

Say I'm the ghost of what I am.
I watched a log-pile turn into a village

with the first ember of morning.
Nobody has to tell me it's illusion.

Low pressure over Voronezh.
The barometer held its breath.

I'm foot-slogging snow drifts
at the edge of the world.

It's a virtual white-out.
Where the paths end up is nobody's business.

Nor where I end up, head down in the water, listening to vast forests grow.

Voronezh, January 1937

The First Circle

A green woodpecker visits my unwalled garden
and begins its rounds. It hacks a slight, millimetering circle
in the lawn, then revolves as though squaring up
to a mathematical problem, one too large for one head,
maybe a problem of style even, to be left in the ground
like a marker of where the matter was left off.

When I left our home for the last time, my head
exploded – as though a rifle had gone off
in the middle distance (maybe she was hiding in our garden;
maybe you had let her know I was coming around).
I had trouble holding myself to the ground; what was up
was I was dead. And this was the first circle.

The woodpecker hammers and scratches the small round
space, I guess, mimicking the hit of rain on a garden:
the way seagulls flamenco on a football pitch's centre-circle
where the least of the action lets the grassblades off.
From the wear of the crimson secondary feathers on its head
the woodpecker is likely to be three years old. It flies up.

I worked up to leaving you over five years. I kept my head,
told you I loved you (and I could not not). I kept it up.
You strayed through our home while I – was underground
all that shift, mining for your grief, watching for that white circle
of air where this labour could stop, where you slip hands for the off
and go from under that ceaseless rain into this garden.

The woodpecker struts back after one hour to its cut circle
and waits for real rain. It seems this animal is all head
and strategy. It seems as patient as a small green general in that garden.
I want to shout, clap my hands, and make its little confidence blow up.
But because the woodpecker has crafted a trap, like a death-trap, on my ground,
because the catch is the beak's eye and art, then I hold off.

I take off my head. It is the same face you kissed as you sloped up
to our bedroom on that last night in our home. And how I ground
into you, knowing next night would be hers. And how I was miles off.
Or how this grief is the age of that woodpecker in the garden,
a problem of style even or of timing for a predator in its circle.
Not you, waiting in the rain in your green coat, when I'd gone ahead

finally into this garden (I made your little confidence blow up).
But that this garden is the first circle; and here, love, is my head
to be left in the ground as a marker for where the matter was left off.

St Lucy's Day

'the year's midnight' – John Donne

Snow wakes you. It flies outside your window.
Fine parallels follow the shuffling cars.
Some sky-god plucks the god-of-all-eiders.
An ice-man instructs the trees to play dead.
Fine parallels follow the shuffling cars.

The weather is a television with its aerial down.
An ice-man instructs the trees to play dead.
Ponds are trapdoors you drop to death through.
The weather is a television with its aerial down.
The angels are above you with CCTV.

Ponds are trapdoors you drop to death through.
Christmas is the madman in red on a snowplough.
The angels are above you with CCTV.
Fir-trees retreat like armies on the snowline.
Christmas is the madman in red on a snowplough.

Your best friends are drunk, adrift in duvets.
Fir-trees retreat like armies on the snowline.
You promise me the whole of white earth if I wake.
My best friends are drunk, adrift in duvets.
Then I walk into the eclipse of St Lucy's Day.

I promise you the whole of white earth if you wake.
Some sky-god will pluck the god-of-all-eiders.
When I walk into that eclipse of St Lucy's Day
Snow will wake you.
It flies outside our window.

Patrìn

or *pateran*,
pyaytrin, or *sikaimasko*.
The marker used by Roma
that tells others of their direction,
often grids of branches or leaf-twists or
bark-binds. Used for passing on news
using prearranged forms, patterns
or permutations of these. Yet
it also means a leaf or,
simply, a page.

Simply, a page
yet it also means a leaf
or permutations of these
using prearranged forms, patterns.
Bark-binds used for passing on news,
often grids of branches or leaf-twists
that tell others of their direction.
The marker used by Roma:
pyaytrin, or *sikaimasko*,
or *pateran*.

Bears

for Gabriel

PawPaw and Paprika, two great bears of the Egyptians
of Lancashire, the Witches' County, Chohawniskey Tem

who, when our camp plucked its tents and pulled out its maps,
walked steadily with the wagons, ambling, always ambling,

all across the open pages of wet England, footing
as far as Pappin-eskey Tem, the flat Duck County,

crossing to Curo-mengreskey Gav, the Boxers' Town;
padded on to Paub-pawnugo Tem, Apple-Water County

as good for bears as for their Gypsy masters, although
who is master is moot after much apple-water;

then to bide by Bokra-mengreskey Tem, Shepherds' County,
for their collies are trained not to bark at bears, but slyly, gently,

slink big-eyed as children behind their shepherd's greeting.

Ambling, bears, always ambling… mooching to Mi-develeskey Tem,
My God's Town, the God for all bears too,

God of paws and padding, of Polar, Kodiak and Koala;
sniffing superiorly through Dinelo Tem, the Fools' County;

circling with our circus to Shammin-engreskey Gav, Chairmakers' Town,
nosing north through Lil-engreskey Gav, a Town Made of Readers,

then paws over eyes for Kaulo Gav, The Black Town;
joy at Jinney-mengreskey Gav, The Sharpers' Town;

to Lancashire as it was then, wider county of white witches,
to the clean camps, to the great brown bears of the Egyptians.

To PawPaw and Paprika, backwards in time they go, pad pad. *Goodbye*.

The bears' route: Lancashire to Lincolnshire to Nottingham to Herefordshire to Sussex to Canterbury through Suffolk to Windsor through Oxford to Birmingham to Manchester and Lancashire.

You Were Broken

for Les Murray

The amazed, massing shade
for the glacial valley, made
by a single araucaria
that smashed its way
by micrometers of birth-push
under five centuries of dusks
of carbon dioxide and rainfall,
while the volcanic rocks made landfall
against its unrolled, harbouring roots;

and the roots took the rocks in their arms
and placed them, magically,
like stone children, about itself
as it unfolded its fabulous tale:
of the wood heart mourned to flint
by slow labour and loneliness,
by what it could not reach, yet see
at distance, and of the sound of that sea,
and of the cruel brightness

of butterflies and grasses,
foreknowledge of their brevity,
of a heard stream, overhearing
prints of otters on its plane stones,
gold wagtails sprying over
the gravel and shallows of courtship;
of orange blames of gall-wasps, honey fungus,
the watch-turning of tree-creepers;
of blights of summer lightning,

of fire damage and that dark
year's mark worn secretly,
a ring, forged inside a ring;
then the winter's coronation closing
in a swaying crown of redwings,
cones, drab diagonals of pine-fall,
the lead winds hardening, and while
the stone children wept with rain
the great tree sheltered them.

Of the Genus *Diatomaceae*

The sea's rooms darken.
Wanting myself dead we watch
from the boat as the billion
iridescent diatoms make
their fleering climb towards night
from the steep of the depths:
that dark, swarming fleet,
every porthole eyed with flame,
lighting now at the form
of a mirrored and a total moon.

Fiction

I was haunted by falsehood from the start, some brink of this reached
by late childhood. To keep lying, to pile it up, was how to live
because fiction tied the parts and parcels of name. Fiction was the poached
life history of travelling folk. Fiction was the electricity and rates.
Paid for your shoes. Fiction took the bus to the store, was allowed
by family law to shoplift. Fiction told the old story every night.
Fiction was poor but dishonest. Fiction gave birth before a grate,
placed my placenta on the sizzling clinkers. Fiction liked comforts.
She had the brains to earn them, but Fiction stayed out late.
Fiction was a virgin before marriage, of course. She laid the hoard
of the tale tall before you. You were bidden to believe in this
despite the fact it was fiction. You had to grow askew. It's hard
quarrelling with Fiction. Because Fiction is you: your bones
are thin beams of fable; and your blood, when it pouts at your lips
draws through its black alley. Fiction has good fingers, she has sewn
then unstitched the same shroud for years. Fiction longs for reunion
with her lover. He died strong and striking. He swam out of turn
down a long and burning sea of blood. Fiction yearned to restring the yarn
for herself, demanded a better ending. Her children learned their part
and played it from affection. But Fiction began to believe her tale.
                    It collapsed into art
in which Fiction was the lead, and her children chapters and verses.
Her friends would spin about her screaming *Author, Author.*
Haunted by so much falsehood, a brink was reached.

Smoke, Mirror

Widowed, one-breasted, Rosa's world had shrunk to Blackpool.
Seventh child of seventh child, she could count on so, so little
except second sight, closed her curtains as though for a passing hearse,
dealt her Tarot cards at neighbours, and sat there, weather-wise.
Picture how a claw hammer angles under a settled nail,
grinds against the top grain, then slides out the clean metal
fresh from first hammering. Rosa works her audience,
and with her claw for grief, she plies her darkened séance.
An unknown sound is ground for a gnomic reading.
Ghosts arrive on time. Her daughter's upstairs frapping
the floor: one tap for 'no', twice for 'yes', with three
slow *bumps* for some spiritualistic ambiguity.
Her son hangs about the back, wanting to beat their lights out,
break wide the curtains, reverse the sham night,
drive out the wake of widowers preening in their desire,
mouthing their childish pleas for another wife and mother.
For Rosa in fact. She squats in her power, plays Gypsy,
terraces a track the family goes up from loyalty to lie:
home as vardo, road as drom, life as one big bengipè.
Her suitors simper. They nose their dregs of tea.
Levering against one man's memories, Rosa overhears the singing
of his dead wife. It's as if Rosa were leaning against air, listening;
as if she were finding the proper angles for that slip soul
fresh from its first making. She drags out the clean metal.

vardo: a Gypsy's cart or caravan; **drom:** a road; **bengipè:** a trick or a quirk

Sèsi o Lety U Písku

I have come a long way and am almost there.
'You were almost there except for this frontier.'
I approach the frontier and see the wire.
'You passed me without looking but I was still present.'
I am almost there except for this frontier.
'There was nothing to stop you yet you rode back to the city.'
You pass me without looking but I am still present.
'Except for the wire there was nothing to stop you.'
There is nothing to stop me yet I ride back to the city.
'You made the brass boast you stopped for one night.'
Except for the wire there is nothing to stop me.
'And you saw this wire. It made you exceptional.'
I make the brass boast I'll stop there one night.
'It made you exceptional. Apart from the others.'
I see that wire. It makes me exceptional.
'Apart from the others, who stared back through the wire.'
It makes me exceptional: apart from the others.
'And you approached the frontier. And saw the wire.'
A part of the others. They stare back through the wire:
You came a long way. You are almost there.

sèsi: a voice

The Boy and the Song

after Celan

The months are hairs combed over each other, or crushed
papers in a cellar. December is growing, fur on my lip.

December's the hair on a monk's fingers, a book pulled open,
a boy throwing snow at the first winter crops. Your hair is twisted up;

it is dark and it makes me imagine shells or cloud-shells, a boat
nudging into a lake under rain. A boat, a book pulled open or over,

fear, a shrew squirming in my fingers… December's black hook.
December's lake water. Can I sing? Can I live through this winter?

A small lyric on my palm. I stand on the shore of a lake.
As far as a boat may be rowed, the colour of aspens

colourless by night as I grow in shade and my age deepens.
I speak of loving you as I speak to you about hands,

shells or clouds. I push the boats with my fingers and they nod
in our bloodstreams, lovers crushed together, or clouds

heaped in a downpour. Walking from the forest I find myself
necklaced with bared hands. December is gaining on me.

Ludus Coventriae

for Isaac

These were marginal people I had met only rarely
And the end of the whole household meant that no grief was seen;
Never have people seemed so absent from their own deaths.

– Roy Fisher

Introduction

This poem tells the story of the city of Coventry's destruction in
World War II. Coventry was one of the leading cultural and trading
centres in medieval England. Its Mystery Plays of that time were
famed throughout the country: Shakespeare is believed to have at-
tended a performance. The plays dramatise episodes from the Bible
and were staged by local trade guilds or 'mysteries'.

The movement 'The Charges on Midsummer Night' uses financial
records of medieval stagecraft for the Mystery Plays in Coventry.
There are three time-frames within the movement 'November the
Fourteenth, Nineteen Forty-one': the morning of 14th November
1941 before the major blitz; the first few seconds of that bombard-
ment; and medieval Coventry at the time of the midsummer Mys-
tery Plays.

On the nights of the World War II raids, radio beams were trans-
mitted from two distant points on the coast of Europe, intersecting
at 90 degrees over Coventry, creating an invisible cross in the sky.
This was used as a precise radar target for the Luftwaffe. The Ger-
man code name for the operation was 'Moonlight Sonata'.

Fifty-six per cent of the city's houses were damaged or destroyed.
The dead and dying lay piled high in temporary morgues, or under
the miles of burning rubble, as rescue squads tried to pull out those
still alive from the debris. Refuges were hit, burying people alive:
'our shelter was like a cage of frightened animals'.

51

The Charges on Midsummer Night

- paid for a pece of tymber for ye Axeltre, & for Nayles for it,
  ye Pagent whereof halfe is to spare in William Catesby's house
- Item payd for Sope for all ye wheeles
- Item payd for 3 Worlds
- Item payd for payntyng Hell Mouth and mendying hyt
- Item payd for openyng and shuttyng the Dores and kypyng the Wynd

- Item payd for settyng the Worlds on ffyer & blacking ye Sowles facys
- Item payd to the 3 damnyd Sowles & 3 Saved Sowles
- Item payd thus to 2 Demens
- Item payd the 2 wormes of Consyens
- Item paid to Death

- Item payd to the Mother of Death
- Item payd ffor a peyre of gloves ffor God
- Payd up also for the gybbyt of Jeiȝe
- Item payd to Mr Fawston for hangyng Judas
- Item paide to Mr Fawston for his Coc-crowyng

- Item payd for 3 Angells
- Item paide ffor wasshyng the Angells surplisses
- Item payd to Iosephe
- Item payd to God
- And also paide to the Spirite of God

- Item payd to Jesus
- Item payd to Mary
- Item payd to Pylate
- Item to the litell dying Chyld
- Item payd for this Prologe

November the Fourteenth, Nineteen Forty-one

Their world, and that of the Catesbys in Cook Street
differed, like
the eggshell hue of the wren and linnet.

o

'Aslepe as Coventree this faire morning'
(the sycamores drip from pressure prior to the eclipse)

whose farms lie smack against canal-basins,
whose long-faced beasts yawn and bask in their midge-clouds

o

So, sleep, as Coventry sleeps this morning
with low sky catching alight from streetlamps.
The sweeping bus views from house to town,
Herod the king, in his raging.

o

Rejoice, rejoice, all that here be!
The angel that has brought this child here.
So now let us all prepare
Our temple and sweep the yards.
God's son who hangs upon the tree
Has cleared away our care.

o

Glossy stare and red squirrel
oblivious in eave or dray
are mass and matter
by close of day.

o

Out of desert, from the hard stone
three air raid wardens run, three kings
late up with pick, spade, lantern,
tracing the star of each explosion and making there.

o

For most stay put,
squat among their own brick and bone
or worse, stray underground
beneath the burning stairs or buried cellar.

o

Behold it has come to pass
That Christ, our just Messiah
Is bought and sold by Judas.
To pacify his father's wrath
He became a man, he ransom pays for man
As he hangs there nailed to the sky. O Lord,
As thou hast bought our hearts
And suffered on high Calvary,
Recomfort us, both slow and spry,
That in thy truth we live and die.

○

Out of danger shall us release.
Out of whose dangers?
The sword or sharpened cross?

It is the bombers' cross-wires
radio-signallers
that drag those planes across.

He is come to set the world on fire.
Red, the town is fallen; alight,
a light; and all its temples fired.

○

With low sky catching alight from streetlamps,
enough light to register from one thousand feet above
nettle-tree architecture of church and spire –
its foreshortened spear, gimlet-eyed cockerel –
sufficient to land on almost, for a horsefly
or a linnet, or firebombs too.

○

The spire writhes in high pressure prior to the eclipse.
Fire-rods brim the blackening moon-circle.

Billy forgets. *This is not the morning after,
it is the morning before.*

Godiva pouts in state from his locker-door.

o

With low sky catching alight from streetlamps
there Billy is, workshying, dribbling a football to the shopfloor.

Inside, the cleaners sluice the floors of its blue dye.

In the yard, rain rinses – 'that's where the foreman Dan
chucked up' – clots of human flesh, eel-flesh, peas, fried potato.

o

Now to receive this king of peace
That out of danger shall us release.
Our high merits shall he increase
In joy abundantly.
For here I keep no more bliss
But that he mark me for one of his,
And then when his sweet will it is
Am I even ready to die.

o

Billy, head-down like a hod of stones after long carrying:
gently and gentled into balance on his pillow; and the day
unloaded stone by stone as though ready for slow walling;
is when he feels the tilt, and the grip goes sliding.

o

Cows clop and gawk
in a blacked-out stall.
Midges struggle, go still
in spider nets on streetlamps.

Sycamores drip. Coventry sleeps.
Sirens wake. Farmers
stare up at stars
moving over their fields into the city.

○

The canal surface shivers
with each detonation.
A bus cuts its lights.
Factories wail. Billy remembers.

His feet slide on his blood.
The Lord is our shelter.
He has come to.
He has come to set the world on fire.

○

Moleskin gloves and polypropylene;   ○   head of a mallard;

pashed dishevelled nest;   ○   cloudburst of milestones;

of frosted manure;
     ○
of buckram coaches flouncing up from the exploding museum;
     ○

pink snow of records (administrative, personal);　　°　　axe of a pub-sign;

 arrows,　apparently human bones;　°
flung gravel: horse-teeth or stun-stones;　　°

°

stethoscopes in showers, and syringes;　°　　　　splatter of Coventry

    Blue dye;　°　　cartoon dancing brickwall;
        °　razed bowling greens;

      strutting graveslabs;　　°　　hail of stained glass;

a child's kaleidoscope: a hatchet;　　　°

a bus hovering in house-high air;　　　°

    its engine bouncing off five walls and still crawling towards Nuneaton.

°

    Park Street ash, and behind that, Pilate
    rinsing his mitts as the crowd thins out.
    We shall show that as we can

    the dog-watch on Trinity and St Michael's
    breaking to wash brick-muck from the corpses.

°

    For their world, and that of the Catesbys in Cook Street
    differed, like
    the eggshell hue of the wren and linnet.

Whitethroat

Whitesmiths work the tinct tin into leaves.
They could weave, if they chose, a whole whitten of it.

It would glitter, that false wayfarer's tree,
as the whitethorn, or the whitethroat calling from its false leaves.

Redpoll

As if she had spilt
from cherries, from holly, from
a shake of nightshade.

Goldcrests

'Cedar-cedar-cedar-cedar-sissu-see' – song of a goldcrest

She sings light, he sings lightly, from the pine-needled nestcup.
He shifts lightly; she shifts light, among the burrs in the nestcup.
How slightly, how very slight, the sky shrinks to their eggshell hue.
How slight, how very slightly, light wakes from their eggshell hue.
He sees lightly, she sees light, in the pine-needle dark.
She sang light, he sang lightly, among the cedars in the dark.

Siskin

on birch and alder

cast between catkins

Kin to the whisper

Kings

for Siobhàn

This here, brothers, sisters, is the title of a book, the head-work of an old king
of Romani land: the Tribunal, or the dispute between
the wise man and the world; or the death-sentence
passed by the soul upon the body.

— from the *Book of the Wisdom of the Egyptians*

Introduction

This poem tells the journeys and trials of a wise fool, a Romani man
maybe more used to the twin worlds of Roma and Gajo than he
will freely allow. He is a fellow-traveller of the blacksmiths' tribe,
the Boorgoodjìdes, useful to them for his part as their shaman.

The poem is a fairytale, once upon a time. The scenes are set in no
country but in many countries the borders of which are invisible.
The time frames coincide with certain events in Eastern Europe,
but the persecution of Roma has been permanent and is a story that
lies outside written histories. Yet the poem is also the man's history
as he remembers it, and sings it.

I

1933

I beg of you believe in the Kings, the blacksmiths' tribe, the Boorgoodjìdes
made up of the tamar, true twisters of sàstra, sras or srastrakàni,

who jam the jagged srast in the jaws, the chamàhoolya,
of their kerpèdy, and ply it, plume it polokès then plakomè

that way and this, rotating it like wire, until it's rinimè, roopoovalò,
arced into white rings, into angroostì, necklaces, into the bright akanootnò.

I am the kings' man, asanòo mànoosh, all smiles, ahmàtsi manoosh…
the kings' fool gadaveskè I bear you belief, forge you four words, shtar hòrata:

four stars to follow: patyàv, apakyàv, patsyàva, or apatyàv. You must pick
or be picked; be picked up or picked off. Like kopanàri, the carver

one choice to your chisel, one sting to your karò, one karò to our thorn.
Asanòo mànoosh, 'all smiles', I can wait for you but, tooryalìste, I circle you.

I am circling you. In the court of the hayfields I am circling you;
in the laws of the hedgerows I run on the field-side, oomalyàkom,

you keeping the drom: I invisible, audible, a flume of finches blowing
through the thornfields at your riding. This conduct I keep for my kings:

heralding them at the sharp cities, their seer, speaker. Tall at fòros-gates
I cry, both falsely and truly: 'Mande will sollohaul neither bango nor tatcho!

Hold the holtà of patsyàva, it should surround you like oopràlyavinate,
be more than a night-belief, a rakyàsapatyàv, or needless nightmare.

Boorgoodjìdes sleep sound in their double-world, graft even in dreams,
                                                            barely bezèti,
for what's righteous in speech, chachoonò, is word-twin for what's real

like their right-wrought srastrakàni, so it is byword with their cshib, their
                                                            chachès…
Now – I bring you, Gajo, to be bridvà, rokker with us, and to deal!'

Boorgoodjìdes: the blacksmiths' tribe; tamar: ironsmiths; sàstra, sras, srastrakàni, srast: iron;
chamàhoolya: jaws; kerpèdy: pliers; polokès: slow; plakomè: squashed, pressed; rinimè: filed;
roopoovalò: silver; angroostì: rings; akanootnò: the present, the contemporary; asanòo
mànoosh: a smiling man; ahmàtsi manoosh: a foolish man; gadaveskè: because; shtar hòrata:
four words; patyàv, apakyàv, patsyàva, or apatyàv: belief; kopanàri: woodcarver; karò: means
both thorn and sting; tooryalìste: circling movement or manoeuvre; oomalyàkom: field; drom:

road; **fòros**: city [or market]; **Mande will sollohaul neither bango nor tatcho**: I swear now
neither falsely nor truly; **holtà**: perimeter; **oopràlyavinate**: sunrise; **rakyàsapatyàv**: night-belief;
bezèti: dream; **chachoonò**: means both righteous and real; **cshib**: tongue; **chachès**: truth; **Gajo**:
non-Romani; **bridvà**: picked; **rokker**: to speak, usually meaning to speak Romani

Night-hosted beneath city walls, our tent posts forestial,
salchinyalò; our hounds hang tense against tying poles,

a hundred hungers of them not counting the tsikooroo zhookels
woofing white clouds as the snow, harèef's heft, lulls against tentflaps.

I slide out to find rum, snow snaring my bootòoshi,
draggling my gait drunk. Guards on the stràha cat-call and caper,

bowl snowballs from high; bury coins in their white breasts.
One soldier holds up a tahtùy of vodka, tries to toss it, gives up trying,

tips the matòo neat on a snowball, doughs it hand to hand
then hurls the hard drink down to me. Kibir kurla? I joke and, Hoolanò!

as I play up the tsirkajìs, half-practising for our tsìrka,
clowning beneath the storm clouds of coin-snow and snow-vodka.

Agor of their watch I have snowballs, but no command,
my tongues are twigs for basket weaving, choochoonya, rayà,

but my jèpa's jammed with ice-hatalì, jingling as I slither
polokès to the tents, kurpìzavà my kaltsa. You have seen me

as I am, dooymooyalò Gajo, dead-legged and dyàslis iphoo,
out cold on my bed with the dark dogs about me. I am summoned,

sovavnò, for bùlnoozyava. The drink holds open doors to my dream,
a lamàda of memory on which the kings scribe their rarorò razprèyzila.

Ahmàtsi manoosh, but this is my mastery. This night I am ready.
I rokker their story back, circling them, track my tale into the gerdèy,

riding the rare roads, until I sleep hòratiba, dream-speaking their romanipè, speaking it plain as I have heard it. Just as I spell this spell: *delpesgodì* –

salchinyalò: branchy; **tsikooroo zhookels**: puppies; **harèef**: ice; **bootòoshi**: boots; **stràha**: wall; **tahtùy**: cup; **matòo**: hard drink, liquor; **kibir kurla?**: what's the price?; **hoolanò**: master; **tsirkajìs**: clown; **tsìrka**: circus; **agor**: at the end; **choochoonya, rayà**: twigs for basket weaving; **jèpa**: pocket; **hatalì**: money; **polokès**: slowly; **kurpìzavà my kaltsa**: to mend my trousers; **dooymooyalò**: double dealer; **Gajo**: non-Romani person; **dyàslis iphoo**: thrown to the ground, KO'ed [wrestler's term: 'give him the ground']; **sovavnò**: sleepy; **bùlnoozyava**: talk in one's sleep; **lamàda**: a flat stone; **rarorò**: dumb; **razprèyzila**: tale; **ahmàtsi manoosh**: a foolish man; **rokker**: talk in Romani; **gerdèy**: gutter; **hòratiba**: speaking: **romanipè**: Roma legend, tradition; **delpesgodì**: to remember

Kings bend about my bed, eavesdrop on my night-speech. Trills and lulls, owlcalls and answerings. The tentpoles wrestling above our canopies

grow woodland in my mind. One blacksmith pours wine, softly; it suggests a strayed stream within me, plying under tree canopies, koonjoopàte, where
it will.

The kings cock their ears for speech of their own species. They hear nothing but my wood-mimicry: retchka and retchko, ràrtigìllichal, a rùkkersamèngri
churring,

kackaràtchi and kàulochìrilo, a weshjook sniffing wiffler, bìttikànni,
bàrripòari...
I am the kings' seer, their bestiary. I am old now; I have many voices in me.

They are patient; they have ridden longer distances than my memory, know I must sing the earth over before I find my sèsi. I burn on this bed.

They lift my lapsed palms, chafe them between locked hands, douse the embers of my eyes with eef, with the skins of iced erikin.

When my arms ignite above me, my watchers sponge them over as if my limbs were lit swords being doused in their making.

Cease snow.   Stream shadow.   Owl now to the owl's hole.
Through the thicket of wood-speech, wildbirds back to their branches:

oopràlyavinate, my chosen hour. It is dawn when my voice breaks:
'There will be a fair in that fòros, races and trading, our stallions steaming

in their stamped paddocks. You will go in the gate with the morning.
Fear nothing save the price of town-charcoal. Fear everything

save the pride of your màstooroos. Leave me now. But leave town by evening.
There is something behind, false water at distance. Prosper, but wear warning.

Where the river rises beyond their stone-ford, a deeper ford is laden
with piled lèshi, shoodrò, some of them limb-slight. I see the faces of
                                                                    children.'

koonjoopàte: in a tangle; **retchka**: duck; **retchko**: drake; **ràrtigìllichal**: nightingale;
rùkkersamèngri: squirrel; **kackaràtchi**: magpie; **kàulochìrilo**: blackbird; **weshjook**: fox; **wiffler**:
pigeon; **bìttikànni**: partridge; **bàrripòari**: peacock; **sèsi**: a voice; **eef**: snow; **erikin**: plum;
oopràlyavinate: sunrise; **fòros**: city; **màstooroos**: mystery, as in the mastery of craft, but also
craftiness; **lèshi**: corpses; **shoodrò**: cold

Sabàlen. The kings are gone. I make my way to the len.
Seven silver shire horses wade, their tails whishing ice-shell in its shallows,

grandfathers in their gravitas. I kick out a wash-pool, yakh of panyalò,
a small eye of water, in which to salve my soldered eyes. An ice-quake

of verglas, a chain of little gunshots; the horses crunch backwards,
backing on to the bryàgoos. There is nobody coming, or watching.

I shave into the moving mirrors of underriver. Randlò, I untether
my light body from its hides and wools, from the skins of surnà,

lathe myself over; let the heat of my dream dry myself before
the cold engulfs me. Only then do I see the kookoochìn aiming

their green darts through the cloths of evènd, the cloths of pàhni,
heads hanging like the erlìdes ashamed of their earliness,

their eagerness to settle. I will not pick these. I will not pick her.
A woman steps over the riverbank, parusyoov melts beneath her

revealing the garavdò, the veiled and unsmelted. I will not remember.
Even as she stands, the light thaw quickens. The horses hove to,

graze at her feet, untethered, knowing her whisper, her weather.
I know only winter, and the tamar, true twisters of the sàstra.

Theirs is my ring now, my field, my bright akanootnò.
But I am not of the tribe. I have neither fathers nor mothers.

I stand outside the town walls with horses and flowers.
I am 'the back one', 'the one behind', the good paloonò,

their teller of futures, rarorikanès, their dreams' traveller.
I watch her ghost kneel among the snowdrop beds by the river.

sabàlen: morning, at daybreak; len: river; yakh: eye; panyalò: water; bryàgoos: riverbank; randlò:
shaved clean; surnà: deer; kookoochìn: snowdrop; evènd: winter; pàhni: frost; erlìdes: Gypsies
living a settled life; parusyoov: slush; garavdò: hidden; sàstra: iron; akanootnò: the present, the
contemporary; paloonò: the back one, the one behind; rarorikanès: mimic and mimicking

II

1905

I dream backwards half my life. The same snowdrops by the river.
I watch her pick a penèrka of flowers before I speak with her.

She will sell these in the city. I tend ten shire-foals, they
with their full maws of shootlyahà, much prone to bengipè,

nibble the air near her, nudging, nosing at the bouquet.
I play host to them, name by name: their mothers and honours,

the pitav of the eldest, tetìki of the tiniest, how any head of theirs
would outpace an ox at the ploughing, izprevarizehìs mìlya!

but their turf will be tougher, to trot behind the talìga,
strung only when they stray, one day to bear the bandrooki,

from follower to followed, bold brasses on their chokàt.
Next time I would boast less. I am at the river next avìn.

We are young; she is twin to both tribes, the city's, the Roma's.
Our early days are bay and roan, the horse-colours of hours

rising into their running-powers. By midsummer I ask her,
win her father's word, my indais kaìli. Our honeymoon

a honeysuckle hooped over a tsàra, an honour-guard of brood-mares.
We wind through the wide land keeping with the blacksmiths,

firing up forges in each gav, shoeing, prising hoof-rot
from a thousand sprinters, pacers and padders. We eavesdrop

word of wars, red guards in sharp cities, but heed to our horsecraft:
foals topple in their birth-ropes, snickering, half-standing;

horses spring from the smiths' grasp as if raring for the racing.
Our camp shimmers with anvils. Hooves flicker on our outfields.

penèrka: basket; **shootlyahà**: sorrel; **bengipè**: tricks, quirks; **pitav**: honesty; **tetìki**: nervousness;
izprevarizehìs: outrun; **mìlya**: a thousand; **talìga**: cart, wagon; **bandrooki**: yoke; **chokàt**:
forehead; **avìn**: dawn, morning; **indais**: tribe; **kaìli**: agreement; **tsàra**: covered wagon; **gav**: village

Reed-birds whose whole lives are spent invisible in rushes,
rigging nests where they will, weaving their worlds from the rayà –

crakes, rails, brown bitterns, whose nests are centres of their earth;
their thin calls correct the spin of the doonyàs: the reed's axis teeters:

everything is in balance. Lift the levels of their lakes, let loose faster foxes
those whole worlds unravel. Rumours ring us; there are red guards

in cities, grey garrisons on the grasslands, and a drought of metal.
We wait on the edges, cry to each other in codes, move only on margins,

unweave our wagon-camps from their usual tsarunò.
Some damn us as daranòok. My young wife sees further.

My beloved spake to me, rise up, my fair one, and come away.
She is white-faced at the kings, a looloodì among thorns.

She takes horse to her city for the feast day of her father
for the evènd is past, the panì is over and gone.

I track her tooryalìste, my horse hammering her hurt grass,
hurt halving me, tearing me, hurling helve after hatchet,

but I cannot catch her. I catch horizons but not her.
Then her city curves into sight; my horse swerves at its river.

Smoke climbs sky-high; flames chew through the rafters.
Red guards race through the roadways, rodav, ratvalilò.

My beloved lies in the reedbeds. The earth melts beneath me
revealing the garavdò, the veiled and unsmelted. Remember.

She is nested in death. I now curse the one who killed her.
Until the day break and the shadows flee away, I balance her body in my arms.

---

rayà: twigs for basket weaving; doonyàs: world; tsarunò: literally 'Gypsy camp style'; daranòok:
cowardly; looloodì: flower; evènd: winter; panì: rain; tooryalìste: circling movement or
manoeuvre; helve: OE: the handle of an axe, chisel, hammer; hurling helve after hatchet: OE
to throw helve after hatchet: 'to risk everything'; rodav: seeking, hunting; ratvalilò: bloody;
garavdò: hidden

My akooshìba: you will meet me in your mirror: you will remember me.
You, who hold the harness of the officers, remember me.

You, who hone their swords on the whetstone, remember me.
You, who swab the shields of the red guard, remember me.

Who rim the rearing wall, rain arrows over our camps, remember me.
You, who cheat our chililgìrs: cavalry, you will remember me.

Who count the cold coin in the keep, remember me.
You, who bait with barvaypì, from a distance, remember me.

Who wall in our wide fields, which slay us so casually, remember me.
Who slew my beloved, slid her to the waters, remember me.

Remember: we are all one: all who are with us are ourselves.
Our word gallops like grass-fires. You will wither by this word.

I will crash through your kingdoms, calling your kanilipè
to the realms of all Roma. I am riding revenge to you,

to the lip and leap of a distant devlèskere pògya.
O dooymooyalò, judge me, but you will remember me.

Hold the halter of patsyàva. I am riding this curse on you.
I wage war with these words, on your raklò and raklì.

Remember I rank you, as shtòopos, as sapnì.
You are ratvalyaràv, randimè. You rise only to be reaped.

Your names now are nangò, your newborn cshoongadimè.
Cshavàlen who chastised us, we who are chindi-chibengoro.

You will remember me. You will meet me in your mirror,
for I am the asking and answering owlcalls of an akooshìba.

---

akooshìba: curse (n); chililgìrs: farriers; barvaypì: riches; kanilipè: evil-doing; devlèskere pògya:
horizon; dooymooyalò: hypocrite, double-dealer; patsyàva: belief; raklò: non-Gypsy boy; raklì:

non-Gypsy girl; **shtòopos**: rubbish, garbage; **sapnì**: snake; **ratvalyaràv**: covered with blood; **randimè**: reaped; **nangò**: naked; **cshoongadimè**: bespattered; **Cshavàlen**: O you people!; **chindi-chibengoro**: without a tongue

La parhoodìlis. Nettle-dew douses the swords of the nettle,
its microscopic thorns are uplifted and sheathed

in incepts of chlorophyll and unwounding serum.
Boorgoodjìdes smash the nettles, simmer funeral zoomì.

So much for weapons. Tsikìnda in the burial yard,
tsikìnda in my buried heart, we bury her by the river;

burn all her belongings, even our bed. I am barèstar.
I opened to my beloved, but my beloved has withdrawn herself.

Even as she lies there, the light thaw quickens. What hard saying?
Fallow luck sees furthest. A heart trammelled or rammed

on its anvil bleeds visions. Get lost. Get lost, boorgoodjìdes.
Ride your mares shoeless. Misplace your atlases.

I am your seer. The herald. Again, the one left behind.
I am not your tame dreamer. I have a horse and a whip.

I have a horse and a whip. I could kill you and go.
I ride by the river, nasvalòo of kamav, kalò with meribè,

tether my horse, and stride straight into the fòros
in the òolitsa, and in the boohlò putèka I seek her,

my ozì piryamlòo. I seek her, amà I do not find her.
But the red soldiers that stand guard on the fòros find me,

they smite me, wound me; for the red guards of the stràha
had taken her veil, her life, from her. What is thy beloved

more than another beloved, o thou fairest among women?
What is thy beloved more than another beloved that thou dost so charge us?

la: her; **parhoodìlis**: burial [performed swiftly after death; because death is perceived as unclean, everything belonging to a dead Romani is burnt, including their caravan or tent]; **boorgoodjìdes**: the blacksmiths' tribe; **zoomì**: soup; **tsikìnda**: nettles; **barèstar**: become stone, made of stone; **nasvalòo**: sick; **kamav**: love; **kalò**: dark; **meribè**: death; **fòros**: city; **òolitsa**: streets; **boohlò**: broad; **putèka**: paths; **ozì**: soul; **piryamlòo**: lover; **amà**: but; **stràha**: wall

III

1933

A garden inclosed is my spouse; a spring shut up, a fountain sealed.
Awake, north wind; and come, thou south; blow upon my garden.

I sleep but my heart waketh. I dream forwards half my life.
Seven shire horses wade, their tails whish ice-shell. Last lilày on this len

we swam a hundred horses, washing the beasts before we bartered them.
How they tantrummed, the stallions and mares, how their manes sprayed

spectra, halo and rainbow. There is something ahead now,
false water at distance. I have always been asleep. How can I wake now?

I have washed my feet. How shall I defile them? I have put off my coat;
how shall I put it on? I rouse again, waking from my last loshalì.

I have been stretched all day in the snow. Sunset stings my eyes.
Flags are flung down, washing poles withdrawn into the eyes of arrow-slits.

Grim gates seal themselves andràl. The drawbridge drags itself up.
Black locks catch on high latches. The city is an anemone, as if a

falling oochipè had run its fingers over its skin. My horses sleep standing.
I feed our hounds on their tying posts. Steppes unravel about me,

the reedbeds shiver with bahtali, with the timid, with garavdò ròmanichìrrilos.
Our camp is empty. They are gone before me. Who will walk out of this
                                                                    wilderness?

I beg of you believe in the Kings, the blacksmiths' tribe, the Boorgoodjìdes
made up of the tamar, true twisters of sàstra, sras or srastrakàni,

who jam the dandalò srast in the jaws, the chamàhoolya, of their kerpèdy,
and ply it, plume it polokès then plakomè rotating the bright akanootnò.

They are gone. Now, seek north wind; and go, thou south; find my people.
A world inclosed is my dream; a spring shut up, and a fountain sealed.

lilày: summer; len; river; loshalì: happiness; andràl: from the inside; oochipè: shadow; bahtali:
white magic; garavdò: hidden; ròmanichìrrilos: water wagtails; Boorgoodjìdes: the blacksmiths'
tribe; tamar: ironsmiths; sàstra, sras, srastrakàni: iron; dandalò: jagged; srast: iron;
chamàhoolya: jaws; kerpèdy: pliers; polokès: slow; plakomè: squashed, pressed; akanootnò; the
present, the contemporary

There is always a drab door to a dookhanì, where plague-carriers
are carried and left alive like a second stràha; always the light lock, or

a skylight smiling open; a little wicked wicker gate, a dooymooyalò on duty,
dead to the doonyàs. There is always a way. I slide into the city

sidelong. Sometimes when I am dreaming, when my kings are khizim,
I dream that I am dreaming and, when waking, dream I am waking.

The city dreams it is dozing, its gullible walls propped on each other;
gutters snoring with water. But something is moving: I run seeking:

I the north wind and south, I am come into this fòros.
A boohaloos arcs along the boohlò putèka, a parnò dìkhiba;

moon clouds release shadow, shadow-dancers, their fallen purlèntas.
I slide through the city, sigyarindòs, so sigòo I reach its bare edges,

71

where nobody sleeps, where nobody lives, where canals in their locks
climb up from the stone-fords, and bright sewage sleeps.

A ràrtigìllichal calls. I reply with wood-speech.
A weshjook barks. I reply with wood-speech.

The boohaloos rotates its white wings and then plunges.
A small cry goes up. The reed's axis teeters.

My kings lie about me. My queens lie about me. They are piled about me.
Shoodrò, they are limb-slight. They have been hiding here all day from me.

Why was I late, who am never late; why am I behind who must herald them.
Their heads are as the most fine gold, their locks black as a raven's.

They are beautiful. They are terrible as an army with banners.
I see the faces of children. I crawl to a willow. I want to touch the one thing
that is alive.

dookhanì: hospital; stràha: wall, a defence wall; dooymooyalò: double-dealer; doonyàs: world;
khizim; gathered; fòros: city; boohaloos: an owl; boohlò: broad; putèka: paths; parnò: white;
dìkhiba: visitation; purlèntas: silk headkerchief; sigyarindòs: hurriedly; sigòo: fast;
ràrtigìllichal: nightingale; weshjook: fox; shoodrò: cold

I wake under the tree. Stars wake above my eyelids as white looladì.
I guide my eye's hand to reach one down, one devletlùki lokò.

The wind plucks at the willow: *there are many voices in me.*
I pick belief, apatyàv. It sings in my palm. It asks only that I follow.

What it says, apatyàv, is that my kings have gone before me.
Sorì simensar sì mèn. I can now go on behind them.

I lie beneath this tree, barely breathing, my body taking root,
my hands wrist-deep in leaves. My spine spindles out

nerves to nettle-root and ragwort-root; they utter to each other.
The skull's crown sinks back as if it were shrugging, or forgetting,

and bright hair clings.　　　－ Sèviba.　　There is thunder.
One raindrop splatters a patrin, o kolè dyoonaste. The chooli's

rain-sisters join in, suicidally, spraying the vùrba with panì on panì
until the willow seems to writhe and whirl, a vertical vurtsimipuy.

I sense her above me, spooling me sastò into del, still dreaming:
Ì am circling you. In the court of the hayfields I am circling you.

You courted me in the lee of hedgerows, running on the field-side,
oomalyàkom, I keeping to the drom: you invisible, audible,

a flume of finches blowing through the thornfields at my riding.
Sov, she says, *drown in me, drawn up on my shelò of shookaripè.*

Address your armagànos to the àngelas, asanòo mànoosh. I am sky-drowned,
her white throat calling——*Te Avel Angle Tute　Te Avel Angle Tute*
　　　　　　　　　　　　　　　　　　Te Avel Angle Tute

so like a birdcall, the redpoll's, my lòlochìrillo, my new wife singing,
and then she is before me, my wife is before me, my love has come for me.

---

looladì: flowers; **devletlùki:** heavenly; **lokò:** light; **apatyàv:** belief; **Sorì simensar sì mèn:** We are all one, all who are with us are ourselves [Romani saying]; **sèviba:** thunder; **patrin:** leaf, also means a page, or a marker left by Roma to tell others of their passing; **o kolè dyoonaste:** beyond, in the other world; **chooli:** drop; **vùrba:** willow; **panì:** rain; **vurtsimipuy:** a whirlpool; **sastò:** whole; **del:** sky, God, heaven; **oomalyàkom:** field; **drom:** road; **sov:** sleep (imp: Sleep!): **shelò:** rope; **shookaripè:** beauty; **armagànos:** gift; **àngelas:** angels; **asanòo mànoosh:** smiling man; **Te Avel Angle Tute:** May This Be Before You; **lòlochìrillo:** redpoll

III

Nightingales

The Gypsies wake in a woodland slown and slurred with snow
their eyes iced shut, fingers counting the cold's cost.
Somebody spades spindrift over the campfire's ghost.
Steam gasps from charred bones, from bone-white embers.

The Gypsies say they spent the night placing pantles for birds,
how they need to nab nightingales to trade at Christmas fairs.
There's a price on the crowns for those minds quick with melodies.
Winter nights in walled towns will ring with their airs.

This is what they say. The Gypsies can't explain the frozen doe.
That tarp must have been blown over her with the snows.
She perished of cold so they helped their knives to her.
They knew the danger, sure. Weren't they sleeping in the dangers?

All this is clishmaclaver to the bailiff and his boys.
The morning drags itself from the far face of a planet.
There are haloes arraying the stares of every star.
Their snow-tracks strike away together before they part.

Chorus
on the birth of Edward

The song-thrush slams down gauntlets on its snail-anvil.
The nightjar murmurs in nightmare. The dawn is the chorus.
The bittern blasts the mists wide with a booming foghorn.
The nuthatch nails another hatch shut. The dawn is the chorus.
The merlin bowls a boomerang over bracken then catches it.
The capercaillie uncorks its bottled throat. The dawn is the chorus.
The treecreeper tips the trees upside down to trick out insects.
The sparrow sorts spare parts on a pavement. The dawn is the chorus.
The hoopoe hoops rainbows over the heath and hedgerows.

The wren runs rings through its throat. The dawn is the chorus.
The turnstones do precisely what is asked of them by name.
The wryneck and stonechats also. The dawn is the chorus.
The buzzards mew and mount up on the thermal's thermometer.
The smew slide on shy woodland water. The dawn is the chorus.
The heron hangs its head before hurling down its guillotine.
The tern twists on tines of two sprung wings. The dawn is the chorus.
The eider shreds its pillows, releases snow flurry after snow flurry.
The avocet unclasps its compass-points. The dawn is the chorus.
The swallow unmakes the spring and names the summer.
The swift sleeps only when it's dead. The dawn is the chorus.
The bullfinches feather-fight the birdbath into a bloodbath.
The wagtail wags a wand then vanishes. The dawn is the chorus.
The corncrake zips its comb on its expert fingertip.
The robin blinks at you for breakfast. The dawn is the chorus.
The rook roots into roadkill for the heart and the hardware.
The tawny owl wakes us to our widowhood. The dawn is the chorus.
The dawn is completely composed. The pens of its beaks are dry.
Day will never sound the same, nor night know which song wakes her.

The Lucy Poem

'Lucy': *Australopithecus afarensis*, 3.2 million years BC

'With rocks, and stones, and trees' – William Wordsworth

As her eyes accommodate
  from the billion-leafed glitter
of deep jungle, the walker
  spies prayed-for water where
the sun bounces like a saiga
  off the savannah.
This is fresh to her:
  to watch forwards rather
than clamber to seek. Sand grains
  slither under her slim feet.

Despite the drowsing civets
  and wild dogs, she steps her
soft track behind her clear
  so her friends might follow.

She can sense as much water
  in her breasts as in the earth;
except there is a denial of water
  even in ground-air: only whorls
of liquefied heat you find above
  elephant-tracks or the tread
of limestone beds. Tiny streams
  start at the hoof point of beasts –
mirages and fractured mirrors.
  On the plain she glimpses
air-rivers and flat inland oceans
  of light above which mountains
flicker: arks of snow wrecked
  on their crowns – the roof
of Africa, sunstruck then shadow-
  halved then forestial
with star-flowers. To her
  those highlands seem
an escape of stone, an island
  blown inland by the simoom,
dust-devils spinning the land
  grain by grain into place.

Her mother's stories tell how
  when those mountains
bloomed from underworld lodes
  springing geladas led their fat
appetites to the snow-caps
  muscled like woolly gods;
and then the gorillas lurched
  through the forests to steal
their high hammocks. Her mother
believes the star-flowers

shrove the geladas, scolded them;
   those monkey-gods were elved now,
scarced in shape. The summits
   themselves diminished too:
they wept so hard they
   no longer kept the season
but wore their water as snow-
   necklaces, ice-pearls…

When the waterhole went
   wolves ran with their thirsts
higher than fur could manage:
   they loped the dry courses
to their source, lapping parched
   stone where water buried its song
and as they pounded upwards
   seeking the wet tongue
of that voice, so the geladas
   skittered, bounding higher
up that mountain roof
   until they regained the snow
and turned to stare
   from its gleaming ridge.

The wolves fathered
   a line of grey wolf-stones
below the snow, staked
   them for years, while below
the plains wilted to sand;
   the forest breathed
its leaf-litter in and out
   until one day it breathed in
maggots and breathed out
   blowflies, and our walker woke.

Overhearing melt-water
   our walker wakes; she balances
her thirst against the night's dew,

steadies herself to the climbing
track, unloads her step behind her
one by one. Shadows moisten
her heeled hollows; the moon's
sun sets her prints as stone,
and she senses herself neither
walk nor walker, striding the hill
in the light of all she knows –
geladas guarding the white
heights; star-flowers
glistening in crevices;
the crouched wall
of wolves;
the high snows,
their wells
of prayed-for
water.

Taken Away

The mother places her baby at the waterfall's brim.
She waits for the moon's climb.

They'd been hard at the hay with a blunt billhook between them
circling and slashing for hours under scything sunlight
with the cradle nestled and nooked on the one hayless place.
They'd had their breakfast, porridge and milk and tea,
scones, cheese, whatever they had. Their picnic things
were scattered on the green knoll around the cradle
as if plates and pots and pans had been tossed out by the baby.

The wife shadows her husband with a wide wooden rake
weaving and whirling his handwork as he worries the hay loose.
You know how a man makes bouts of hay with a scythe

and round and round the field in close and closing spirals
he rounds on the hayless knoll and that one white cradle
with cups and greaseproof wrappings pallid with butter;
like a maze of mauve leading into a green eye and an unseen
staring gap among the eye's blades. Some small wind shoves
the grass as if a snake were sidling.

                                  The parents are heads down.
Their muscles move with each other as if they were making love.
Round he goes, and round she goes, a buzzard's marriage
on a thermal. Then a cry goes up as if the soil were screaming
or the wind were wounded on nails of brittle straw. A cry
neither parent has heard and cannot stem with any known thing,
not milk or love or kiss or words or food. The young doctor
from across the glen hears the child's call across five miles.
He rides towards it as if the cry were a fire rising in the fields
but all his knowledge's clear water will not quench the child.

And so it goes for the fever of three thickening months
except at the wick of midnight when the baby closes down
as if his switches had been thrown, or some wires scissored
in his throat. Tethered by their child, the parents thaw into sleep
only to freeze awake at dawn as the cry bursts back alight.
Folk keep away. Folk catch that cry in their cattle's eyes; taste
its scum in their milk and mutton.

                              At summer's flow, the postman
deaf with listening to a lifetime's stories, strode into their cottage,
downed a dram, and drank the scene into his memory: salt water
damming a child's throat, a cry that would not cease for love.
He stayed with him all day. The parents scrammed for provisions
and the cure of quiet. As the door slammed and their footfalls
slapped into the lane, the postman turned to the baby and the baby
sat up asking if they had gone and, if his parents had gone
would that now mean he could get up at last – and get up he did
as if he were a young man sternly sick of his own board and bed.
He could stand and speak. The child's voice was dark and thrown
as if four corners of the room were talking with him or through him.
The child clenched the whiskey bottle and downed enough to throw
a horse. He drew a long straw and slit it to the note of a flute.

Then he played the long day through, making the postman drink
deeper and harder than he had the head or height or heart for.

A moon widened on the windows; a garden gate squeaked
cringing on its hinges; the parents poured through the door
to find their child crying in his cot like a seal left on some low ledge
of the Atlantic; and the postman pointing at him, adrift or bereft.
'He's not here, your child. He's not anywhere. He's taken away.
He told me everything, how you left him to the cloud and sky,
left him to the harebell and the grasshopper and the cow parsley,
left him in grazed gaps between grass, to skylark and to hoverfly,
while you worked, if that's what you were doing.'
                                        They knew
one cure, one pure matter passed from their grandmothers.
When midnight massed itself over breakers and shore,
when the tide of the day had flown, mother, father and friend
headed by torchlight up the headstream on the high moor.

The mother slides her fairy-baby towards the waterfall's brink,
taut-shawled, his baby arms pinioned like a wrapped cat.
The child's mewling, breathing the breath of the chilled spray
slaping up from the trout-brown pool at the fall's foot.
The father and their friend are behind her, egging her on,
baying that it's for the best, that their child isn't in the child.
The moon bends a bow behind a cloud-castle then shoots
its light-arrow through a slit across the waterfall's rim.

The Circling Game

John hammered and hammered hell-hot iron on his anvil.
Work was slow in the water that summer so what work he had

he struck more art into it. These horseshoes were a set, a double-set,
a dapper pattern, a gift for some girl he had long had his eye on.

There was a slap at the open smithy door and in loped
this lad, not more than sixteen by his skin and under his arm

a woman all wrought wrong like she'd been raddled under a wagon.
The lad asked, 'Let me a loan of the fire, bellows, anvil and hammers;

and let me work here alone.' Later the lad looked in on John.
The girl had been made right. She looked more than mended.

John fetched five guineas from him for that fire and free hour.
'But don't be doing as you spy others doing. The tatcho drom

to be a jinney-mengro is to shoon, dick and rig in zi,' the lad warned
holding the girl's arm as he left. John had a mind to try the lad's trick,

so tranced up he was by the art of it. He sized up his fresh horseshoes,
squinted through the nail-eyes, all over their harped, heavy angles.

Those shoes might have proved half the art he needed for love
but John had a hidden, beaten shame in him – a hair-wide snick

in his soul's steel. He couldn't court the girl with such work.
He doused the smithy-fire, hooped the eight hot rings on a wire

with his hope and walked across the valley to the town for a drink.

A fair was in town. There were posters tigering the shop-windows
and streetlamps. A horse-river ripped through lanes and ginnels.

Cobbles chuckled, shined under that iron tide. Street-silt, sheep-muck
and salt-grit from a slown winter shook up dust devils and mare's tails.

Rainbow tents and caravans flowered in the river-meadows.
John ran through them to hear their colours, to smell canvas slapping,

guy-ropes springing and pinging on pleached pegs, wounding
scents of grasses into his nostrils, making the penned ponies slaver.

John strove to stand square, to glimpse between dazzling horsecloths,
for there were horses here that John might as well imagine as see

– Andalusians, Spanish Barbs, Lipizzans, Camargues –
three thousand or more with their masters and flexing foals.

And children. The streams, the becks, the waterfalling children
bucketing like water from slamming caravan doors. The horse fair

ran with children. One sleet shout could freeze them before
they thawed to laughter. John looked out over the fair's field.

He thought he was witnessing the world or one bright field of it
with old counties buried but still breathing beneath counties.

When work was slow in the water you could go and come and go
through the mirrors of these fairs. John's hammer and hardware

hung jangling on his work-belt. There was always luck to a fair.

The fair roved every other week. It was as if the tall tents tucked
up their skirts and scuttled from one field to another. So quick

and sprack and spry were these moonlit flits from village to village
the tent-pegs had barely pushed down a first root before being plucked.

The Gypsies' wagons evicted curlews from their sites. For two weeks
they havered within hearing of each other. The sorrow-flutes

85

of the birds bubbled and purled over fenland and moorland.
Three skiving summer months John wrestled with, then won,

the trust of the hooves of high horses. For the shyer creatures
he played them the circling game – the send, the allow and the bring back –

then they'd nuzzle him softly for sugar and his salve for whip-cuts.
That gave John the nod of the horse masters, and means for meals,

yet money flapped about the fair, not a note of it settling near John.
He could sniff the stuff wodged in the pockets of the masters' jackets:

brash, burnished bundles of cash for buying up ponies on the spot.
The masters stank of rancid bank-notes. Their palms were plummy.

Their palms were planed purple with done deals and sure things.
John played a circling game with the horse masters, sending

himself off when wanted most, shying on the end of a lunge line
of their flattery, letting himself be talked back to the fair with a drink

before coming back and laying out the tackle and terms of his trade.

The horse masters answered to no man but their king, a Gypsy himself
who joined John as he worked, enjoying the sound and sight of skill.

As the days drew on, and John's silence drew him, the king spoke
of his own pain: how last summer his shire horses shied at an adder,

casting their wagon with his one daughter inside it, how since then
she was broken in body, blunt and blind. John asked to take a look.

The daughter was wrought wrong and John thirsted to find favour.
Months back, John had watched that lad gain a girl from the dead

with fire and hammer. He'd spied the lot through an eye-high knot
in the wood grain of the smithy door that he'd knocked out so

John could keep a look-out on customers with fast fingers. John coaxed
the king's pain from him with a promise he might mend the daughter,

remake her whole. And if he did, the king said, John might be more
than a brother to the tribe and king. The daughter was given

mashed poppies: stewed slurring flowers in a steaming steel mug
that slid her to sleep. Father and masters kept vigil in their vardos.

All night John had his furnace flaring, its bellows rasping and blasting.
The daughter's body flamed and melted. Her hair fled, flew up. By dawn

she was all dust. John poured her ash across the anvil. He palmed it,
gathered it, chopped and hammered it. John spat and mixed and waited.

He remembered he could barely remember a word that lad had said.

Cockerels were volleying vowels from valley to valley. John sensed
snaps and snags of twigs as deer drew darkly back into the woods.

The furnace grew cool and quiet. The daughter's ashes were damp.
John was weeping. He was already dead. He listened to the world waking,

eavesdropped dawn's massacres hooked in an owl's eyes. Below
cold clay's skin, moles waged war on each other, twittering, brawling

as blind as worms in their looped, lapsed trenches. John parleyed
with the silence with prayers. The dust stirred on the anvil's altar.

Blackbirds and thrushes broke their voices in the blue darkness
between tree canopies. Dunnocks drew bows in their throats

and fired music through the walls all around the silent smithy.
John knew in his mind there were nouns to each sound, prayers

in their pattern, noise with no name in the ear's echoing chambers.
What speck of the lad's spell had John not spoken? The daughter

was dust. Her ashes on the anvil were asking and answering him.
Then John heard a knock nagging at some distant door.

In leaped the young lad as though through the bare wall
beside the winking anvil. He blinked at John's work as if he were

staring through the blacksmith, sighting his soul's hair-wide snick:
'Man, it's not her. It's you need the mending. Didn't I tell you

not to do what you spied me do? Down tools and watch my work.'

The lad plied the daughter's dust and blew over those grains
until they glowed, embering on the anvil as the lad let slip

sharp sure calls, kind words and calm words. Shamed, John slid
towards the door wandering, still weeping. The lad turned on John,

'Man, go home and give yourself to a girl who can melt and mend
the tears in you. Love's the craft of it. The fire from its flint can bend

and make anything find fresh form. But let love circle you, mind.
Love's no shying horse for the asking and the shoeing. Send

love from you, as you have, and it will not allow that nor come back.'
As he said this the daughter's dust sparked. It spoored up between

the lad's arms as he lent art and shape. The daughter woke, melted
into life, leaning into the lad's neck, breathing his known name.

No Gypsy noticed John as he left, his tools still sulking in his hands.
When John reached home he gloomed for three months, then rose,

woke the flames of his furnace and frenzied a glow with his bellows.
Work was work, but what work he had he struck a lighter heart into it.

He sized up the old horseshoes, squinnying through the nail-eyes,
all over their harped, heavy angles. They were a set, a double set

88

with a circling pattern, a gift for a girl he had long ago had his eye on. John tipped and hammered and tapped those deft shoes on his anvil.

Sunlight leant through the open smithy door and in strode the girl.

'The tatcho drom to be a jinney-mengro is to shoon, dick and rig in zi': 'the true way to be a wise man is to hear, see and bear in mind'.

The Library Beneath the Harp

Papusza

Bronisława Wajs, 1910–1987

At thirteen years old I was skinny, as nimble as a wood squirrel only I was black. I read books. My fellow Gypsies laughed at me for that. They spat at Papusza. They chirred about Papusza. *Your name means doll. You are a reading doll!*

I asked my family to enrol me in school. *Please, you a Gypsy girl and you want to be a teacher?* I asked schoolchildren to show me to shape letters. I always stole something and slipped it to them. Not far from us lived a Jewish shop-keeper. I stole a chicken for her. She showed me to shape words.

Years later, some Gypsies were playing music on a farm by a river and my step-father took me with him. As I walked I sang, 'The water does not look behind. It flees, runs farther away, where eyes will not see her, the water wanders.'

While the Gypsies played their instruments, I read a book. Some gajo, Ficowski by name, sneered over to me and spoke: *Well, well. A Gypsy – and she can read! Now there's a surprise. I heard your lovely lament. I've been following your voice work.*

Papusza burst out laughing but I had tears in my eyes. He smiled. I showed him my songs. I sang my world. Ficowski said Papusza was something his people must hear. He said this so carefully Papusza almost loved herself. Her tears began falling in herself all for herself.

I approached the abyss. I told him about Papusza.
How it was raining. It was raining in her underworld.

gajo: non-Romani

Songs of Papusza

I was once besotted with a black-eyed boy. The young men
of my kumpania stretched him out in an àshariba. Only then

did Dionýzy Wajs, ancient Dionýzy Wajs, pay his coin and court.
He possessed harps, bought my mother and stepfather's heart.

All I possessed were secret books. Dionýzy arranged my bed
as we both wished. There will be no children, he had said.

This is what I swan-sang when I wed: *I am marrying
his harp.* I died back to life as a child, a bride at fifteen.

I heart-sang *The harp is the abyss. I shall never know
the earth again, not through her notes, not as the notes*

*from a thrush's three-fluted throat, or notes of rain
from a wrung spring sky, not notes of my horse's strain*

*as she clamps and cleaves the clogged road. I am nothing
but these fingers, fronds furling over a harp string:*

*those springing strings in my throat where the wind
of my breath wakes poems.* So the roads unwound,

my beloved books sly in an oilcloth beneath the harp
like prize tools you'd want wiped, spry and sharp;

and my voice swivelled, swelled, stammered on her song
while old man Dionýzy Wajs stretched and struck at his strings.

àshariba: a wrestling match; **kumpania**: a band of families travelling with horses and in caravan

Dionýzy Wajs folds his harpist's fingers, the fingerprints
wasp-stung while strumming his shimmers and feints

throughout the forest-villages of Volhynia. Our harps
are hauled upright over our wagons, like rigged ships

of music moving on breezes between those little ports.
Skilled mistrals finger the strings through starless nights.

We travel all day. We pay back the night with our numbers.
I sing at the dark while Dionýzy Wajs flickers and flexes.

My husband's harp hangs on a high hook. He tensions
the strings to one fugal tonne of force. He polishes

the teeth of its buzzing bray pins, the plane of strings
perfectly perpendicular to the soundboard. I sing

and his fingers follow me, melody murmuring on a thread.
He tilts the forepillar like a sight from which he can read

my every glance. A fleshy pluck, he says, will wake the warm
wan note; while a pluck from the finger's bone-tip releases

that strong, strewn soundburst: a drum's boom across the wires;
a door deepening on darkness; our windows as the winds slam.

At each stop we bartered my threnodies and melodies
for the orts of oats, lines for linen, for a mew of news.

In these villages, nothing happened but our music
until the Germans came. They murdered the menfolk.

We Gypsies couldn't flee for fear, nor fiddle for food.
We freed our nags from our carts. We wove into the wood

those heavy harps banging on our backs. We trickled into trees.
No water, no fire; hungers tensioning across frames and faces.

Chased by Ukrainian bandits, one Gypsy lad laid his harp's head
to the lie of the land. From that shallow sniper's nest, he shouted,

'We'll shoot all of you with this carbine!' And those bold bandits
outgunned by his humming harp, scampered downhill like rabbits.

Then a German came to see us: 'I have bad news for you.
They want to kill you tonight. Don't tell anybody but I too

am a dark Gypsy of your blood. God help you in the hell
of this black forest.' Having said this he embraced us all.

Everything was rags. We yearned to drink from the Milky Way.
Only the river learned of our lament, and maybe the sky.

For two then three days, no food. All slowed sleep-hungry.
Unable to die, we stared at the moon… I curse-sang silently

Ah, you, my little star. At dawn you are immense. Blind our enemy.
So the Jewish and Gypsy child can live, confuse him, err him astray.

Whose eyes saw us as enemies? Whose mouths cursed us?
Do not hear them, God, I cry-sang out to the night. *Hear us.*

On such a dark hark of frost a little daughter dies.
Over four days, mothers fold four small sons into the snows.

92

All the birds were praying for our children. Numb night came.
Old Gypsy women death-sang their fairy tale: *Golden winter will come.*

*Snow, like little stars, will cover the earth, the hands. Black eyes will freeze,
the hearts will die.* So much snow; it buried the women's warm bodies.

Years later, the moon shook in my window. She didn't let me sleep.
Someone looked inside. I dark-sang, *Who is come crying my kinship?*

*Open the door, my dark Gypsy. Open the window where it bangs and glows,
where shapes with shovels are slamming and slotting the locks on savage doors.*

*You have come only for bed, for that would be bread enough.
You have come only for my song, for that would be dream enough.*

Ice-lakes lapse. Linnets alight on flicked and flickering branches.
A lone lizard waits. Women from a village woke us from our trances

whispering that a war was won. We spied down to the valleys
where falcons flung their talons into the meadow's nurseries.

Family by family the kumpania fossicked from the forest's shadow.
We lit our first campfires. Nobody bombarded us from below.

Last year, I was panicked through a summer-sly woodland, chased
on three flanks by fascists. I kicked forwards at the softest pace

arrowing my feet between the pine cones' grenades, those hair-triggering
twigs. Hovering on haunches, I placed my held harp against living

bark before tip-touching the forest's floor with my fingerprints.
As if dipped in iron filings, manacled by a million tiny pincers,

wood-ants wove their ropes up my arms and neck, tilting me nestwards
with the harp's heaving wood a fat feast for these workers.

I ran and the red-hot ants hung from me as they tore at the territories
of skin and hair… Now we are told: it is spring again. The valleys

of Volhynia and Poland are veiled under dust from half-treads and tanks.
A red army climbs in a column. The linnets listen in their branches.

Havering hare, worn low by a hundred hidden harms,
I want to paw into the earth, lie fallow in my form.

The woodlands and plains were singing. The river and I sang
our notes as one word after another, the river stones enjambing,

poring over the poems of itself in whorls and whirlpools. Free to sing
we parleyed through broken Poland, the Red Guards punctuating

our road's unravelling story. For years my voice burst their barriers. I sang
in bribe as well as rhyme. I sang in time and I was always smiling

although my song was frozen as those buried children; although my song
whiplashed with woe and the whickering drones of the dead waking

as if blown back crawling from their bone-ash to my resurrecting song.
Unnoticed, we were noticed. Unwritten, we were written. That spring

I started placing my poems into printed pages, sheaves of silent song.
A gajo, Ficowski, plucked my poems from my throat as I was singing

and those children, grey-faced in green graves, broke into song.
How that cold country listened! How the grim guards started staring!

Sealing them into a book, Ficowski's ink dripped over my songs
prising them into his pages' prisons – mute, unmoving.

Ficowski's key clattered in its lock. His footsteps fell away. I sang
to no-one in the night of that book's covers, but I sang Papusza's Songs.

In this spell of a song there is a speck of poison. In that poison
lurks the white space of a lie. In the lie there is a proposition.

In the proposition – a blurt of blood; a dagger driven –
What is the Gypsy Question? asks nobody yet the question is asked again.

Papusza's poems point out that her people are problems for the gajo.
Like a victim seeking celebrity in his sainthood, Ficowski says so.

Those Gypsies should settle, they should be gouged from their vile vardos.
They have endured enough. Listen to Papusza. Ficowski says so.

Someone close to you betrays you so casually, believing himself
a favour-framer, a fame-thrower. I am called before the Council,

the Gypsy Kris, for my sin against the tribe. Here, I say, are crimes:
I longed for love; I longed to live; and I longed to read and rhyme.

I looked to the first too bitterly; to the second too slightly; and
to the third blindly. Love-thrawn, death-drawn, word-blind

I stand before you willing it your wish that I be cleansed
of all my songs and shames and poems and books and pens.

vardo: a Gypsy's cart or caravan

The straw on which a Romani gives birth is burnt. A Gypsy dies;
the caravan with all goods and clothes is flashed into flames.

They're unclean. It's unclean to step over a hammer or scissors;
unclean to defile cookware with a cloth for cleansing the floor.

These things are burnt or thrown away. You cannot live unclean.
Dionýzy Wajs sits behind the Kris, unstrung, his white hair hanging down.

His caravan and carved harps are on fire; the scorched strings whine.
The chief Gypsy stares past me. His decision: *mahrimé*: unclean.

My tribe treads around me. The Gypsy children chirr like squirrels,
Your name is Papusza. Your name means doll. You are a reading doll!

I am beyond my kind, beyond kindness.

My heart is hewn in half.

Now that you know me you do

not know me. Listen to the harp:

There is Papusza who sings for you

and Papusza who sings for her kind.

Now there is invisible, cursed Papusza

stuttering on a stick through Poland.

You cannot write of Papusza.

She is without language or kumpania.

These are stuffed in her mouth:

a sickle, a hammer, a word-dagger.

There is nothing to be said of her

and less to be written or heard

or her own curse will course through you

even after Papusza curls up cold.

This is my answer to my enemies.

I am stained and unstrung:

your ink etched in every fingerprint;

my nails, their moons eclipsed

in your ink; each tendon torn, untethered

from its bone's bond. I grasp

this pen, and it ungrasps my fingers

as if I moved it with my mind.

Who is this nurse with her notes

her knives? I snatch at a hard hand

but it is already wriggled from its wrist.

Electricity earths through me;

I writhe on its bright rope's end.

Bronisława Wajs, can you still hear me?

The doctor said this so carefully

Papusza almost loved herself.

The doctor smiles. My tears begin

falling in myself all for myself.

It is raining in the underworld. I stare back through a staring star.
I approach the abyss with my husband's harp. I shall tell him about Papusza.

A Lit Circle

All the world was inside this ring and the ring inside this yet

Inside, horses are slamming their heads and hooves against the canvas wall.
Outside, the canvas is red muscle rippling with their massed force.

Inside, the horses ram and rebound from the tent's strained skin
their nostrils flushed flared, their tails tapering under the heat.

Outside, the sky's firing rain as grape-shot, raking hedgerows,
knifing nests from branches, lopping leaves, exploding full flowers.

Inside, it's raining fire-balls from the big top. The king and queen poles
blacken, primed to blow up or flash-flame. Outside is waterfalling rain,

is edging across the floodplains, is mirror spilling out more and more
mirror all along the errors of dammed ditches, choked flood-drains.

Inside, the horses are seizure and slaver. Scenting the rain maddens them.
They try to hide, to vanish among each other, into each other. Outside,

the first fists of flame fling gold into the rain, into what will quench and quell.
Inside is escapeless, airless. *Outside*, the horses start screaming. *Outside.*

Rom the Ringmaster

Do you nav cavacoi a weilgorus? I call this a fair. Ratfelo rinkeno weilgorus
cav acoi:

you might chiv lis sore drey teero putsi. One poor farmer's pocket of soil
but we've long pockets. You know farmers. Once, Gypsies were of use.
Harvest-time. Hedge-laying. Now they've JCBs, migrant crews, gangmasters.
Those fields we fetched our caravans to, they're blocked off now.

Farmers take six or seven big old bins crammed with concrete, hardcore,
then JCB the bins into a block our vans can't jab round, not without a scratch

so we don't bother. When they wanted us, farmers left the country on a latch:
lane-gates and field-gates, front doors, even their larders and ladies.

What's gone's goodwill along with the work. Gypsies blame the migrants.
White work-shy folks blame both. Round it goes, this hate, hurtling around.
The question is where's that hate going to hurtle when it's without home,
when there's no tober to tie the big top to, or job to keep the baby in the
bathwater?

But this field's ours for a fortnight. This is where wide England will walk,
squat itself down then watch us and wonder. Here, around this circle of grass.

Do you nav cavacoi a weilgorus? Ratfelo rinkeno weilgorus cav acoi: you might chiv lis sore
drey teero putsi: 'Do you call this a fair? A very pretty fair is this: you might put it all into your
pocket': a Romani saying from the *Book of the Wisdom of the Egyptians*; **tober**: a circus ground –
'tober' is *Parlari*, the British circus language which is partly derived from Romani and is not a
written language.

Zhivàkos the Horseman

This circle of grass needs to be sited just right – superlevel, softhard,
southnorth.
Horses are picky. Shires, Shetlands, they've attitude just like you and me.
Making circus isn't about our own people's pleasures, not when there are beasts.
Beasts come first and last. On a one to ten the horses are eleven, twelve.
We've a camel too, scatty skutsome creature, who thinks she's horse.

The circle needs to be compass-correct, that means me standing centre
while the ringmaster strides around me with string and a hundred stakes
one hammered in every two paces, every two paces one hammered in.

Then we rig everything around the ringside in old order, the big tent,
four king poles, twelve queen poles, all the spaghetti of the electrics,
spotlights, winches, pulleys, the silver thread, stalls, circle, costumes, mirrors…

Then we might think about eating unless the animals need foddering first
which falls to me and my boy who's over there with his whip. That's him
snicking grass from the ground, from its sockets. That's his first trick.
In a year my boy'll have twenty tricks. Then he'll be after my act.

skutsome: sharp

Demelza Do-It-All

After my act as barrel-walker there's my turn on the silver thread, more subtle
than my turn with those fantailed doves, dementing dogs or hoop-hurling.
I do ten acts solo, six more with my sister starring as *The Starlight Sisters*.

I look in that mirror with that big hundred-watter and I don't know myself.

That's eleven different names, that's sixteen costume changes and they say
we don't work hard. That's what the police said when they gave the Court
                                                                        Order.
'Left the matter in our hands.' One day's notice to strike camp and shove off.

The act with the glitterball, that's my favourite, when I'm up in that steel star
swirling sixty spins a minute for a full two minutes, and that glitterball's
spattering silver stars over my body until I'm almost imaginary. Dazzling.

What's hardest is a hurt, sprains say, crying cramped in the caravan for weeks
overhearing applause from the canvas through the open door, that's pain,
or hearing the claps of rain on the van's roof when the show's over.

I was down in the industrial estate with my sister for small animal food,
the vet for the dogs. There are swastikas scratched on every circus poster.

Colin Clown

On every circus poster, let's face it, my face. Not Mick's face. Not Mike's face.
Why is that? Is it because I am so handsome? You can say that again. Is it
because I am so handsome? There's international clown code in that decision.
Each clown has his face painted on to an eggshell and no two eggs are alike.
Which is why I'm up in lights on the town's lampposts and not Mick or Mike.

I've heard some horror stories about this town. Have you heard the one
about the bent coppers? In the end they used pliers. I've been promoted.
Mick and Mike got nabbed with their mitts in the mopus, so. I am Pierrot.

Arlecchino, Pierrot and Auguste. Mike and Mick swiped the first parts
but I was an august Auguste. I was the straight man the audience likes
who catches the first pie or bucket but doesn't pine or make a racket.

I am Arlecchino. Where is Auguste now? I am afraid of Mick and Mike
but their faces lied. They work somewhere dead now. Like Shropshire.

What's that noise? Is the cat at the door or the wind? Or the wind's cats?
My face is clean. My hands are clean. I'm dead. It's raining dogs out there.

Harlò the Watchman

Dogs out there are clamouring. Half the night they've lurched on their leashes.
I'd call the police if it weren't for the coppers lurking out there, off-duty.
I've spied their ski-masks. Seen the bushes bob and shift as they size us up.
Watched a squad car swallow its blind eye, bringing in supplies,
baseball bats, bike chains, burgers, the like. They're counting us up
while drumming up their numbers. That's the grapevine, the buzherimos
down the pubs. Not every gajo loathes a Gypsy. Not when they're circus.

Long nights are long nets catching bats, bats catching moths and me
watching, catching everything, drinking, watching. Watching headlights
squirming around the roundabout before stopping, dimming, winking.
I don't like the bushes shifting. I don't want to go where my thoughts
move with bushes. Half of me wants the rumble, the other half is running.

I've no tricks, you see, no act. White lie. I had an act, half an act counting
my brother. But you can't catch me now, brother, as I rise into the air
from my trapeze. You were flying to me, grinning, when both of us caught air.

buzherimos: gossip; **gajo**: non-Romani

Kasheskoro the Carpenter

Caught air. Caught light. Caught art. Caught sound. Caught song.
A circus catches the lot in one lit circle. And who makes it, mends it,
lights and strikes it? Nobody rigs a rope and tackle like Kasheskoro!

They approach me with the parley of a day's pay. *Can this be done?*
It cannot be done, not without miracle, balance and my just-right joint.
Structure stretches on a thread. It streams across air that billows

with damage. So: I plane and saw, saw and plane. Chamfer. Dovetail.
I say to them the wide world whirls on a thread. Health's on a thread.
Wage is on a thread. Friendship, loyalty, love. They all need craft.

What I need is MDF, meticulous method, and then you're laughing.
Then you'll have your illusion that Demelza's dangling by her teeth;
that the clown's taking flight even though he's as fat as the big top.

My trick is to make centimetre-certain none of you are caught out
or take the big drop, or flip the wrong flop. Nobody must know
that their dream depends on the dovetails and details of Kasheskoro.

Stiptsàr the Stilt-man

Kasheskoro upped
and offed at dawn
taking his toolkit
and trade, not waiting
on his wage. A plain
van came down on
the camp skidding shyly
on the frost, window
down. White words
were spoken. Birds
cued up their chorus.
One cigarette, and
the carpenter was gone,
sawdust still stuck
to his stockinged feet.
We're down three men.
Mike and Mick were
given the shove.
Somebody is counting
us down. I see all this
in my stride, hear all
this from below, where
my false shoes show
under those pinstripes

like drainpipes. Trust
me. There is a talent
to being tall. Why is
the stilt-man trusted?
I am the accountant.
Every pang of change
in the till, every page
of banknote, I feel and
read. Even the Ring-
master asks about pension
contributions and percent-
ages. I'm careful. If I
stumble once, that's
thirty-five feet of falling
man at ninety degrees
to the second. I back-
calculate my steps to
the inch. I toe this
dotted line. I worship
these numbers and
have given my word.
There's no door I can
enter without humbling
myself before God.

Mashkàr the Magician

Before God as my witness, on the tip of every one of my fingers
perch firebirds. You cannot see them, but listen. Close your eyes.
Hear their burning plumage. Smell the fumes of flaring wings.
Excellent. Now, open your eyes wider than a child on her birthday.

Do you not see crimson gifts? What are you waiting for? Flight?

We rehearse hard until we can play it blindfold in a dreamworld.
Watch as I wake this white kitten from my wrist, this burst of birds

from my breast, this absolute arrow in my heart. Mysteries.
Miracles. Marvels. Mashkàr, where did I lose my wand this time?

I play my audience lightly. I carry them home in my magic cases.
I make as if I don't care. I am weeping yet you will not smell tears.
Here's my cape and cane. Here are two traps, and a trapdoor.
Here's my map and plan. What is your name, Sir? I can find you
your future. You will die, Sir. No, Sir. Not me, Sir. Now, Madame?

I am talking to the space where their eyes will tear into time.

Saydimè the Strongman

Tear into time? Me-karèste!
                          I can tear into these phone-books, run a rhino
on a lunge-line, cart this caravan till Christmas.
                          I pelt through my stunts solo,
eke some strength out for the first night and go out running.
                          Zhivàkos's
leading his horses in, all the Shetlands, Shires and big Arabs. Night rain's
stuttering on the big top as I go.
                          That's when the masked guys strike,
when me and Kash are out of frame.
                          That's who they were waiting for,
to bust from the bushes, lob five, six firebombs through the flaps, then
wrap the tent with its own ropes like wrapping meat in an earth-oven.

They're popping pictures with their phones, not that they have fingers
for figs when I light on them.
                          Not that they don't crap themselves
when Kash veers up in that van.
                          The canvas is caved-in candle-mess,
locking the beasts in, gluing the flaps shut and whoever else's trapped there.

I aim my arms at the entrance. Like fork-lifting two tons of terror it tears.

Horses pour past me into rain carrying me on their shoulders.

Me-karèste!: Big deal! [Literally, 'That's on top of my penis']

103

Moolò the Musician

Where's Moolò? Here's Moolò. Why are you calling when I am here
where I always go, stage-left of ringside with my tin cymbal, snare drum,

tin whistle, my sweet loops of music, my white lies of sound that make
the big top vibrate or slow to silence when the silver thread's being strode?

Under my thumb the beat of the red drum and the applause ripening.

Woodpigeons unhinge from the hedgerows. Where the beasts were bedded
there are scraps spilled from the floors of heaven. Magpies spy and spring.

Curlews collect long keys to their low homes between the burnt grass.
Lapwings manage their manic marriages, low-diving, upside-downing.

One trodden ring. Yellow grass. Green grass. Black grass. Where's Moolò?

*I am here where I always go, stage-left
of ringside with my tin cymbal,
snare drum, tin whistle.
Under my thumb
the beat of the
red drum*

and the applause of wide England where beasts come first and last.

Here you are standing centre.   Here, in this circle of grass.
Caught song, caught sound, caught art, caught light, caught air.

The stage-names of some of the circus people are taken from Bulgarian Gypsy dialects. **Rom:**
true Gypsy; **Zhivàkos:** quicksilver; **Harlò:** sword; **Kasheskoro:** wood-worker; **Stiptsàr:** miser;
Mashkàr: the centre; **Saydimè:** respected; **Moolò:** dead man

Skeleton Bride

Light up, phabaràv, kindle the kind wood
for the rose of the moon is opened; the camp
nested in darkness; our dogs snore in their heap.
Prala, you are chilled. Seal your eyes when you will.
Those lamenting tents might then fall silent.
Our women are waiting on your rule of sleep.
Here, take my blanket stitched with flame.
Weave what warmth you can from what I say.
Keep listening, more like overhearing I know.
Don't heed the wind's gossip in the trees. Those elms
lie. Oaks over-elaborate. I have coppiced them all
for my word fires. Here is an ember to light you.

Here is a story to return you to the surface of earth.

This happened to me and it didn't happen to me
or I spied it when I only heard it or found it
when it was given me through a greater grief.
Remember the creatures we crave as children,
living things we crush in our craftless hands? –
canaries in a cage we spatter with gravel,
conies we caress before trampling them? Well
there was this Gypsy girl, Vogi, all of fifteen.
Her father had snared her, body and soul,
clasped her as viciously as his own widowhood.
They travelled narrow lanes, shy of thoroughfares.
Forced into the open at horse-fairs, he forged
foul lies about Vogi's wiles before striking camp.

Their vardo fell under a fly-cloud of suitors,
none of her father's favour, each a horsefly
parched for the bloodmeal of a dowry. They rode
head down, hardened to the nail of the road.
Some of these lads stole, some moonlighted – bad jobs;
each had winter in their sights, with its clearer aim.

The father set sly tasks, testing them, or spun twisted
tales about his daughter. One by one, they dropped;
man for man he swatted them; but after each fair
a boolòti buzzed in the wake of their caravan's wheels.
Marriage had to happen; marriage had to make a shape –
'a sharper shape than horseflies'. The father put it about
that at the midwinter horse fair he would sell Vogi.

There was spindrift on that flint lake for the fair; an ice lid
a yard thick, and one thousand wagons moored on it.
Bonfires startled themselves into life, their hearts raging
boiling the ice below. As more vardos moved in
to make camp, depth-charges blew under skidding
wheels, hooves. Tench, trout, char woke lightless, peering
up through strange skylights hacked out by horseshoe,
hammers and the raging of those bonfire suns.
By the glowing midnight, that lake was a lava-mouth
on the mountain, its summit blacked-out. Violins fizzed
in the fists of masters; banknotes spat from palm to palm;
horses shuddered then slept as the whisper was given them.
Vogi watched, knowing the meaning of the following morning.

Deadheaded, her father slept, a ringing vodka bottle
trophied on his chest. By late sunrise, Vogi
hared the high crossways striking for the city.
Splattered, manured, those high hidden roads unrolled
their trades, beasts, traffic. A ptarmigan warned, creaking
cackling, descending the snow on its stiff-sheeted wings,
a whiteness on whiteness. Those wheeling clouds, the hills
revolved around her as she paced westward. When the rain
rammed her, Vogi cupped her palms and mouth, became a well
flooding and clearing. When the headwinds harried her,
Vogi steadied herself. She held the hand of the hail.
Two bear shapes watched her from a bivouac's hollow.
Then they stood their whole height becoming bear and man.

In her freefall through frost, through drawn limbs of the ling;
through closed lids of harebells, through ribs of white roots,
through green shafts of sphagnum, black spoils of peat hags,

through undercrofts of moss, through the eyes of worm holes,
through the dead back of bedrock to earth's weeping chambers,
the bear-men gorged on her gifts: touch torn from her fingers –
the men ripped those golden rings; plucked her hearing
with two hands; scent and song taken with her tongue
with what she could not see. And what Vogi could not see
with her tongue were her song and scent in her hands
with a pluck of sounds beyond sense: their breathing hard
within her, with hard bear-laughter, their shoes rasping on road.
Glaciers grinding and bending around her forever, and then never.

No speech as the search party slung the calfskin on to the ice;
nothing for a wandering ear to seize on and shape for a voice.
No say. The sticks and rings of stones where tents were struck
spoke: shadow-fires of camp-fires circled Vogi's body. No wake
then but a watch: widows cast behind to see the site made clear.
Vogi's body stripped, shaken over with shale-oil and what her father
pitched through the hole of his vardo's door: two dresses
mazed with mildew, a bible, a baby's blue bonnet. Half-fires
were dragged, swept together to make a farewell on the ice where
before leaving, Vogi was tugged and dumped, the surface so bare
now after deep firing it slopped on its hasps. The widows knotted
guy-stones and flax ropes to Vogi's white wrists, folded her into the fire
then poled down until the ice-hearth tilted and whalebacked over.

Vogi rides that upturned boat of flame as it bows to the lake-bed
trailing whispers, cinders: sharp signals flaring to violet then out.
A fire's weight of light. Green gravities in that freezing water.
Vogi scuds the lake's floor, sends sand singing around the wreckage,
floats on her flax ropes swimming at nothing, the only currents
the currents of an eel's wake; rushes of debris in open mouths of larvae.
Slowly they awaken around her, drawn by her shadow where
all is shadow: *Watch a door opening in the dark above you*
as though you and I had been buried together without knowing how.
To wake. To reach out and find you beside me when I thought
I had lost you; that I was never to be allowed one more sight.
Not only a door but our windows wide with life; wake now and rise
for they have risen towards you, they have reached out and released you.

107

Vogi woke unbound, undrowning her breath against the weight
of water. She kicked and swum, tides passing through open bones,
gained the roof of ice, clawed until she gripped the brink
of that fire-hole and hauled up on one finger. Unbelieving,
laughing at the flax ropes eaten to bone, Vogi stared at the pebbles
of her feet, the rigging of ribs; held her bright skull and laughed:
laughed the rain's music, laughed stones skittered on an iron river,
laughed hagfish, larvae, laughed a squall of blackflies, mayflies,
laughed invisible waterfalls swelling underground after sharp showers.
And when this laughter was out, when this laughter flew up,
when it swelled within her and grew its own soul,
as if laughter held its own gravity and drew a world closer,
Vogi found herself standing and not hurting, and whole.

The snowline. As though a sea of summer air shored there,
shed its jade driftwood and withdrew. Scrub, gorse and fir
were bent into a springing dome, thatched with thick ferns.
Vogi worked the wood, marvelling at the latched precisions
of tree grain, knot and wood ring. The forest fed her. The forest
folded her into arms of roots while the roots' tongues whispered
to the lake below, taking in her story as slowly as a year's water.
The word of her fluted from woodcock to woodlark. Even a river
caught it, winding the word of her like a whisper between boulders
or a thrown voice within waterfalls. Pine martens snatched the word
of her like bouncing prey, bore it down the stairs of the mountain
to their young; and when the mountain was slown down, when winter
shred the forest, the word of her word wound into the ear of her people.

Vogi woke and rose from her home of stitched branches. Foresters.
Gypsies. Axes. They were a world away yet they were here before her.
They stared through her. Vogi smiled. She could hear everything;
even their thoughts were sullen streams from which she could drink,
cupping her mind into dream and fear. They feared her. Vogi smiled.
Her calm collapsed them. *Unravelled by your hands I am mended.*
I am broken beyond breaking. It has rained tears all year. The land
is sea on which the earth's floe is a raft far off course. All it takes
is one word of wind to snap this woodland from its mooring. The lake
is my daya, the forest my dado, I call on wind, my phen, for this word.

Vogi strode to the men, and through them. Axes crashed on air. She smiled
and they woke in their lit tents and houses. This happened to me.
I saw and heard her. She gave me this gift through her greater grief.

Even now, when rains ram her Vogi cups her palms
and mouth and becomes a well flooding and clearing;
when headwinds harry her, Vogi steadies herself;
she holds the hand of the wind; she strides into the earth's
floodplains and windplains; where the world tilts
at lake's edge or river's rim, she sets her body to that slant;
she watches how the weathers weave her, broken beyond breaking.
The rose of the moon opens; she clasps it, cuts it,
she folds it into her hair. Vogi found her way home
by making a home of her body that had neither the ropes
of muscle or the silk of blood, nor a whit of thread
or mort of mortar. She holds most as she holds least:
up from earth's centre she rose before me, unravelled by the road.

Here, take my hand stitched with flame. I am burnt low.
Weave what you can from what I have given you.
Prala, you are warmed; the corpse-candle is dying down.
We left part of the world, brother, behind us on the road
when, tonight we traversed those woods, saw the hoods
and hooks of rooks and corbies twisting and bouncing
around the lynching ropes. Those carcases cawing in the trees,
they were our hanging brothers. We stripped them rightly.
We cannot strip their wrong. Seal your eyes now.
Seal your mind's eyes too. That sight had cut you down.
Let the fire flicker out, the flame tongues fall down.
Let my hand of sleep close the whole moon's flower.

Let your hand of sleep close the whole moon's flower.

phabaràv: to create light; prala: brother; **Vogi**: the soul; **vardo**: a Gypsy's cart or caravan; **boolòti**:
cloud; **daya**: mother; **dado**: father; **phen**: sister

IV

The Invisible Gift

John Clare weaves English words into a nest
and in the cup he stipples rhyme, like mud,
to clutch the shape of something he can hold
but not yet hear; and in the hollow of his hearing,
he feathers a space with a down of verbs
and nouns heads-up. There. Clare lays it down
and nestles over its forming sound: taps and lilts,
the steady knocking of the nib on his hand until
it hatches softly beneath him. And when he peers
below his palm, he spies its eyes, hears its peeps,
but does not know yet what to think. He strokes
its tottering yolk-wet crown; feels a nip against
his thumb, buds of muscle springy at the wing, and all
the hungers of the world to come for this small singing.

The Boy and the Wren

In as much as anything is anything
this is an invisible universe, yet particles
in his fingers swirl within Saturn's rings,
they fly in the eye of Jupiter and arc
across the Great Galaxy of Andromeda.
This is not poetry. It is mathematics
in as much as anybody is listening.

In as much as anybody is listening
the lorikeets and redpolls trill
imperceptibly as if the sound
of our planet had swung to zero.
Nothing is happening and no one
and nothing is calling and calling
in as much as anyone is listening.

In as much as anyone is listening
the boy vanishes through a door
while his parents shout and snarl
the words none should hear
while a child is in hearing.
This is not history. It is every evening
in as much as anybody is listening.

In as much as anybody is listening
the boy grows tired with running
when a bush bursts open before him
to reveal a wren rampant in song
and everything is forgotten
that needs to be forgotten
in as much as anything is forgotten.

Ballad of the Moon, Moon

El aire la vela, vela.
El aire la está velando.

after Lorca

A pettelengra boy whacks petalos on his anvil.
   The moon slides into his smithy, bright as a borì.
The boy cannot stop himself staring. The moon
   releases her arms in flames of flamenco,
her sweet dress slipping from one shoulder.
   'Nash nash, choon, nash nash, choon, choon.
If the Rom catches you he will splice your zi.
   He will smelt your soul for miriklè and vongustrì.'
The moon smiles, 'Chavvo, let me kur my kellipen.
   By the cherris the gyppos come, they will find you
poggadi on the anvil with your biddi yokkers lelled.'
   'Nash nash, choon, nash nash, choon, choon.

Run for it, moon, run away, moon, fair moon.
  I can hear the hooves of my horse masters hammering.'

'Chavvo, muk me be. Don't pirro upon my pawni
  ringi so rinkana.' The drumskin of the plains thrums
with hoof-strokes. The boy backs across the smithy.
  Horse masters hove through the night-tree
a forest in slow motion, bronze and dream.
  Bronze and dream are the Roma, their eyes sky-high,
their gaze lances through walls of world and smithy.
  But the moon dances her prey to the snare of a mirror.
She hauls the pettelengra o kolè dyoonaste to the pliashka.
  The Gypsies ride at her trailing veils, her mokkadi doovàki.
The wind whips by, wraps the moon in her purlènta.
  It wraps that bride, the moon, the moon, *barval, bevvali!*

pettelengra: blacksmith; petalos: horseshoes; borì: bride; nash: run away!; choon: moon; Rom:
Romanies; zi: heart, soul; miriklè: necklaces; vongustrì: rings; Chavvo: boy; kur my kellipen: do
my dancing; cherris: time; poggadi: broken; biddi: tiny; yokkers: eyes; lelled: locked up; muk:
let/allow; pirro: tread; pawni: whiteness; ringi: dressed; rinkana: spruce; o kolè dyoonaste:
beyond, in the other world; pliashka: Romani ceremony before wedding; purlènta: silk
headkerchief; mokkadi: dirty; doovàki: veil; barval, bevvali: wind

Gypsy Ballad

after Lorca

Noon buzzes with blowflies,
the microcircuitry of cicadas.
Two gypsy tribes ride into a ravine,
ramming into each other
the bull's head of their battle
smashing about the coppice
stamping, slicing like a rutting bull
mounting his own horns.
Two widows watch weeping
from beside an olive net.

The gypsies are down or out,
nine are dying and dead:
Juan Antonio spews scarlet lilies,
the spume of pomegranates.
Sunlight slits the ridden
and the riders to silhouettes.
The gypsies dream of snow
and bandages as they bleed
and sweat. The women
crouch low. Angels of dust
eavesdrop from above.
A mob boss and his henchmen
step out from the olive grove.
'Gentlemen, you can trust
these people to do this
again and again. Four
Roma leaders are dead
and five more of their best men.
These fools do our job for us.
Finish them and fleece them.'

from The Gypsy and the Poet

Finished planting my ariculas – went a botanising after ferns and orchises and caught a cold in the wet grass which has made me as bad as ever – got the tune of 'highland Mary' from Wisdom Smith a gipsey and pricked another sweet tune without name as he fiddled it

John Clare, journal entry

> I hid my love when young till I
> Couldn't bear the buzzing of a fly;
> I hid my love to my despite
> Till I could not bear to look at light:
> I dare not gaze upon her face
> But left her memory in each place;
> Where'er I saw a wild flower lie
> I kissed and bade my love goodbye.

John Clare

Wisdom Smith Pitches his Bender on Emmonsales Heath, 1819

> Wisdom leans against an ash tree, shouldering his violin,
> slipping the bow to stroke the strings that stay silent
> at distance. All John Clare hears is a heron's cranking
> and the frozen bog creaking beneath his tread
> until that ash tree bows with fieldfares and redwings
> and the birds' tunes rise up and twine with Wisdom's.
> The men gossip an hour and John Clare writes down
> the tune 'Highland Mary' and the Gypsy's given names.
> Once Clare is gone the birds refasten to the ash-crown.
> Wisdom hacks and stamps the heather beneath his tent,
> claps a blanket on springy furze to serve as mattress
> and hooks a nodding kettle to the kettle-iron.
> He hangs his head, listens, and shoulders the violin.
> By practice and by pricking to mind he will master this.

The Ditch

As John Clare rises from the ditch where he writes,
frogs bob up through duckweed and roll their eyelids.
The poet's coat and hat, they thought, *were rain-clouds.*
The scribbling pen and riffling paper: they were the rain.
The cloud and rain have moved like lovers out of sight.
Woodlice wake under bark. Nests nudge from within.
Buds are easter-hedged with eggs. A world unwinds
unwinding a world: hedges are easter-egged with buds;
woodlice wake under nests; bark nudges from within;
the lovers and rain move like clouds out of sight;
a scribbling paper and riffling rain: they are the pen;
a thought's hat and coat and rain-cloud: they are poets;
frogs roll up through duckweed and bob their eyelids.
And John Clare settles down by a ditch, where he writes.

Magpies

'This atrosious tribe of wandering vagabonds ought
to be made outlaws and exterminated from the earth' –
A Clergyman Writes. John Clare strides to Emmonsales Heath
with the poisonous passage. Wisdom lights his pipe with it.
'Spark one up for yourself, brother, but don't scorch a sonnet
by mistake.' (Clare is scribbling lines on the brim of his hat,
his paper riffling in the breeze). 'My dad said all along:
when the Gentile way of living and the Gypsy way of living
come together, well, that is anything but a good way of living;
except for riming and your botanising and your good pie, poet…'
Two jabbing magpies strut about the camp on a pin-prick search.
'Take those twin piebald preachers begging for our bread.
They would pick out our eyes and hearts were we lying dead.
All that holds them off is life. The grave is an empty church.'

A Walk

John Clare has cider; Wisdom Smith has loaves and cheddar.
They both have good legs. Nine miles of heath and heather
to heaven and nine miles home. By noon they are soaked
and sheltering under one of Wisdom's sprung willow benders.
'You say you want leaving alone to get on with riming,
that you need a house for the task, with British oaks
for a roof and the best of slate on that.' John is writing.
'That light-tailed foal there. See how she lolls in wet grass.
Blue-bottles and horse-flies let her be to roll or doze
she not smelling of fear or love or any such daftnesses.'
But John cannot warm to April squalls under canvas.
He pockets his poem. 'I know no more than a child, John,
but I know what to know and this is home.' Clare bows
to the Gypsy; the Gypsy to Clare. 'Where is my home, Wisdom?'

The Gypsy's Evening Blaze

John Clare picks at Wisdom's tobacco pouch:
'Kindness flows like water in Christendom.
Wait –' the poet writes 'while I pen a sketch.'
'I am no fit subject, friend,' warns Wisdom.
'To me, friend, this scene is wild and pleasing.'
'To you – *friend* – whose nose is nibbed with teasing.'
'To me – friend – so strong the scene prevades:
Grant me this life – thou spirit of the shades!'
'This is clishmaclaver. Cease feigning, John.'
The friends sit, hushed. Their pipes glare in the dark.
'Take my baccy but do not write me down.
Gifts given and ungiven are like words
forgiven and unforgiven. Word for word
they leave signs. I will not leave one boot mark.'

Wisdom Smith Shows John Clare the Right Notes and the Wrong

John Clare hails Wisdom Smith. The campfire leaps and licks
around a pot of hare stew. 'Timing again, poet,' notes Wisdom.
Afterwards, with quids of tobacco turning in their cheeks
the Gypsy lilts and spills notes on his fiddle. 'There are some – ,'
begins Wisdom, 'some that shall stay – nameless for shame –
who think our – music degraded when, in fact – it is the Deepest
of the Deep.' And the Gypsy slides his bow like a single scissored
screech to drive the point. Clare wakes up with a jolt and a jest,
'And there are plenty who say that about my poetry, Wisdom.
Why are the wrongest notes nearly always the rightest?'
Then Wisdom Smith plays him a melody no one alive has heard
not even the player, and Clare's mind clambers through crevasses
and canopies with only the Gypsy's fingertip holds for a guide.
'It is not deep, John,' says Wisdom finally, 'it is all surfaces.'

First Love

'You were saying, friend, you were children together,
larking with this girlfriend Mary in the church yard?'
John Clare flushes, 'We were playing at being birds,
fetching seeds and rosehips for our hidden brood.
I threw a walnut that struck Mary in the eye.
She wept and I hid my sorrow and my fancy
together under the shame of not showing regret
lest others might laugh it into love.' The Gypsy
stands, stretches and sets down another basket.
His palms and fingers bleed. 'This is the art of it.
If only we had craft like this for love, brother.'
Wisdom Smith squats in his nest of willow baskets,
each basket a perfect wicker creel. He twists and frets
the wands, not once glancing at the weeping poet.

Mad

Wisdom Smith smiles into his steaming bowl: 'March Hares
grow spooked in their bouts, so tranced by their boxing,
you can pluck them into a sack by the wands of their ears!'
John Clare hungers. He hugs his bowl and starts writing
on the surface of the stew with a spoon. 'Let the hare cool
on the night wind,' urges the Gypsy, 'Sip him but do not speak.'
The moon uncovers her face; the men slumber with minds awake –
for the stew has another mind and unpours the bowls into the pot,
shivering to stillness on a dying blaze until the broth is springwater
and hanks, ribs and lanky legs that dress themselves in bloody fur;
then a living hare leaps from the pot, dancing around Gypsy and poet
who, for this moment before morning, are asleep in the great spell
and who dream of striding backwards to Emmonsales Heath
to where mad hares spar and clash over the surface of the earth.

English

'Your language, Gypsy,' mocks John Clare, 'is borrowed goods
or burglary. You smash up English to be hardly understood
then dispart under the drowk of your dark tongue's dossities.'
'And you?' smiles Wisdom, 'Folks say you dine on dictionaries
yet you remain a blank child, as foal-minded as any of my ponies –
tethered by a line, you still nose and slurp at flowers and clovers.'
But his friend is no longer listening to him: he dythers in miracles –
glimpt hedges are freshing with roosting starnels; a whirlipuff reels
as if something danced in it, and tazzles the grasses, ruffs the corn
where its wands are ramping, strows and stirtles the sprotes upon
the spirey blaze as the Gypsy progs it, forcing sparks with a stickle
to twinkle from the flaze. 'Gently now, brother,' urges the Gypsy,
'Warm your mind before you write of the things you see or hear.
They might not be of this world.' 'But my words are,' breathes Clare.

The Hedgehog

John Clare is in a brown huff. Wisdom Smith is boxing the air,
prancing about him like a stoat. 'Poets are prickly creatures,'
jabs Wisdom, 'for all your talk of not having a second skin.'
'So Gypsies are whey-eyed, one-faced simpletons?' sulks Clare,
'Never an enigmatic word! Hearts fairly leaping off their sleeves!'
'I should skin you alive for that,' scowls the Gypsy, 'Slit your throat,
singe, gut and truss you like a pullet; wrap your poet's spiky pelt
in thumb-thick clay and plumb you into a fire-pit. Pluck clay
from your roasted trunk and serve up the dish called poetry:
all heart and squashy muscles.' Clare bunches himself into a ball:
'I would bind myself so tight, brother, I would never unroll.'
'If a hedgehog will not uncurl we pop him in a pot of hot water.'
The Gypsy springs at the poet. The poet rabbit-punches him in the gut.
Wisdom is winded and laughing. Clare grabs the kettle and runs for it.

Second Love

The Gypsy snares a warren with a snigger of wires.
John Clare gropes around the coney holes for rhyme.
'You seem out of mind, poet, or out of time.
Are rhymes caught like a martin gaping for flies?
You to your work, brother-gaper, and me to mine
but no sobbing if supper is two bare bowls.'
They sally across the heathland to his camp. 'Soul's
Breath,' gasps Clare. A woman, waist-high in flowers.
A flash to a flaming. 'Do not stare at her,' cries Wisdom.
His friend climbs a doddered tree and clings to its crownless tip.
'You will seem a dotterel to that girl, brother,' caws the Gypsy,
'Loon-minded and limed on the branches of whim.'
John Clare is wordless. He is watching poetry from a tree.
A poem moving through wildflowers. A poem that will not stop.

A Spring Wife

if I had taken a step with out this caution
my love would have met a sudden end

The hedgerows itch with last summer's nests;
unwise saplings try bright buds on their wrists.
John Clare is climbing the pollard to the sky.
'What do we see,' pants Clare, 'when we espy
a young woman cross a field?' 'You mean to say –
"What does John Clare, Poet and Lover", see? –
what I see are manners on the gallows,' sighs the Gypsy,
'We should go before we are caught and mocked.'
A thousand fieldfares lift off from the shocked
uplifted arms of an unleafed, woken oak.
'The Spring's spry wheels are rhyming on the roads,'
cries Wisdom, 'down the highway of every hedgerow;
and the birds from the North are steering with the sun,'
'Time,' shouts John, 'to declare.' And he climbs down.

Poems Descriptive of Rural Life and Scenery

Wisdom Smith reads; mouthing each murky word
and slitting his knife down uncut pages – *skrip-skrip*.
'If you will take it,' mumbles Clare, 'it is yours to keep.'
'And if I do not,' snips the Gypsy, 'it kindles firewood.'
Wisdom frowns: 'This – "mystery of common things" –
wagtails and nosegays – snowdrops and shepherds.
Who would buy and bow over – well – what he can read
by simply staring about the world? And – seeing
as most eyes are struck from their sockets by poverty,
who has the will to squander time on poetry?'
John Clare deals the cards: slap-slap-slap-slap, slap.
'I fear, John, you are writing for squires and their ladies.'
The poet nods at no one. He flips his cards face-up.
'No,' smiles Clare, 'I am not. I am writing. For my Mary.'

A Steeple-Climber

The Blue Bell Inn on Woodgate in the small hours after Time.
'I was thinking,' slurs John Clare, 'now I can turn a poem
I might turn to an even thornier art.' 'Like hedge-laying
you mean?' winks Wisdom, 'There is more coin in snedding
than blotting.' 'My friend, there are men of merit and name
who pleach whole hedges of words. They call it criticism.
What I want' – Clare pounds the deal table – 'is more scale.'
Mishearing, the landlord stumps across with a brimming jug.
'I just mean,' stammers John, 'to be taken to heart by those men.
I have been a steeple-climber all my life. Such is my poor pen.'
John glares into his ale. Wisdom flickers a finger toward the ceiling.
He blows a slow column of smoke up. Everybody in the pub
stares and sees what the Gypsy has made. '*There* is the steeple.
This' – Wisdom circles his arm – 'this is the church and the people.'

Bender

'Let us relate our stocious tales of last night!' John Clare howls
and Wisdom hoots at the memory of them fleeing – filching
a lanthorn and a flagon of ale then dossing and drinking
until dawn in a ramshackle shack which, by the morning,
had completely caved in around them. 'We were like barn owls
on a beam,' cries the poet, 'outstaring, upstanding!' 'You, brother,'
tuts the Gypsy, 'are still drunk or, any road, drunk on some idea.'
'It is the poetry of night, Wisdom. That is the very barn you Gypsies
used for your reveries and romancing.' 'It is where we slept, brother.
But it is a singing summer. We will wind willows into benders.'
'Poetry is in season,' laughs John, 'Rooms woven from wound wood
are like rooms of woven words.' Wisdom looks at Clare – hard.
'Poetry is not everything. You know that, John,' smiles the Gypsy.
'You are wrong,' dances Clare. 'Everything. Everything is poetry.'

My Children

The Gypsy progs the slow fire and listens.
'I do not write,' John Clare tells Wisdom Smith,
'my fingers founder on raising a pen;
'my eye blackens the parlour and the hearth;
'all I love – hedges and fields, stand silent;
'I have no pride in working or in life;
'I no longer have a friend in yourself;
'I have no friend in myself'. 'I had children,'
breathes Wisdom, 'all three boys now dead or grown.
I was a boy myself when fathering them.
Those boys.' The Gypsy rises and stares at John:
'Don't – don't stamp on yourself.' 'Every moment
I stamp on myself. Were poems children
I should stamp their lives out.' 'Then do not make them.'

Worlds

'There is nothing in books on this,' cries Clare.
'I do not read, brother,' states Wisdom smiling,
'for I will not bother with Mystery.
Worlds move underfoot. Where lives Poetry?
Look,' hums Wisdom Smith, 'in the inner domes
of ghost orchids – how the buzzing rimers
read light with their tongues; or in this anthill –
nameless draughtsmen crafting low rooms, drawing
no fame – except the ravening yaffle,
or fledgy starlings bathing in their crawl.
I see these worlds – lit worlds. I live by them.'
The wood-ants sting. John Clare shifts foot to foot:
'I did not know you gave me any thought.'
'This? All this – is nothing, John,' laughs Wisdom.

Hedge-layers

Sheep scuttle from pasture to pasture following their green god.
John and Wisdom go gapping-up: one man on the cattle-side,
one among barley; both friends shin-deep in sliding cherry mud.
Their billhooks snicker as they sned the stems and the stubs
weep sap. They have toiled since dawn. It is time for their bait.
'It is time for debate,' shouts the Gypsy over the hazel hethering.
'We weave the pleachers later.' John Clare kneels at the feet
of the hedgerow. He sheep-shoves through one of the breaks;
his body will not follow. Wisdom smiles and goes on speaking:
'The hedges of hawthorn yearn to become trees. They grow
with their young legs splayed. They sway with ripening buds.
A pleacher reaches for its root through its bark and sapwood
which is all in our cut and our angle and our taking of its toe.
Lie fallow there, poet, and you will grow young with the hedgerow.'

The Souls

'Hark,' chaffs Wisdom, 'while I show you the craft! –
each rock's snug square on its brothers' shoulders;
their boys – those bitty stones – they huddle under.
Capstones? They're the boss. Boss-stones man the edge.
Now you choose the stones, brother, while I graft.'
Clare stares over the vanished field of sedge.
'It's for a wage, John. What is land to me?
The road is my pocket. Yours is poetry.
When winter comes it is walling feeds you up.
High walls shield you for when you have to stop.'
But Clare has downed his tools. He strides unseen
under the wall, beneath the moors and sky
below the scum of ditches, and between
his soul and his old soul's following eye.

Hunters

Wisdom Smith whets his knife; John Clare oils his tongue.
Starlight reaches them after a million years of flying.
'The night makes a promising page,' murmurs Wisdom,
'You trance your rhymes like moths under your lanthorn.
I trap the nibbling deer with wires and soundless blade.'
'When I was a boy,' shivers John Clare, 'Why, I dared
never look up in my wanderings; my eye ever glegging
under my hat at every stir of a leaf or murmur of wind.'
'Poor John,' whistles the Gypsy, 'a quaking thistle would
make you swoon.' 'Truth is, Wisdom, a thistle still could!'
laughs the poet. And the friends snort and drink to the night.
Clare snores beneath his blanket. Wisdom rises from the earth.
Their fire is all there is to show. Orion stares down on the heath.
He searches for their world with a slow sword of light.

A Bivouac

'I love it when fieldfares flicker and chinking redwings steer
between stars': John Clare gazes up from the fire
tuning his stare to starlight. Wisdom hushes him, 'Brother,
we cannot nap on the wing like the swifts or the swallows.
There is legwork at dawn down the limekilns at Casterton.'
'The night lets slip her mind, Gypsy,' starts Clare, 'She hears
in light. The dumb, dark matter we conceive of as night
is where we hide or are hidden from the poetry of her thought…'
'And there is the poetry of dreams,' growls the Gypsy – 'John,
when you say her, you do mean him, don't you? As in Him?'
'I do not care what to think,' Clare mumbles to Wisdom.
'Henceforth,' declares the poet, drowsing, 'I shall not think twice.'
'No, you shall think twice. Twice.' – and the Gypsy rolls his eyes
or his eye rolls him; as he turns the world, or the world turns him.

The Ring

The Flowerpot Inn at Tickencote. The lime-burners slake
the Sunday through, dousing quicklime from their lungs.
Wisdom coughs; John Clare mutters: 'Again we are owls –
hacking up pellets of ancient bone and stone. Pour me a lake
of beer to plash my innards of dust.' 'Lime torches our tongues,
brother,' wheezes Wisdom – 'no lake large enough for a poet's.'
His friend charges him. The Gypsy dodges. John goes sprawling.
'Why, brother-labourer, what is askew with your bearing?
Why do you spill in the sawdust with skidding feet?
The flags of a common inn are no place for a poet.'
John Clare stops larking. He stares weeping at the walls:
'My wedding ring is lost, gone in sawdust or the kiln coals.
I was never married, Wisdom, not unless I were wed
to my first wife and first love and first everything. Yet she is dead.'

The Friend of All Friends

'I walked the hard road home with my garrison, Wisdom.
I had my invisible army about me, all of us hungering.
I gained Northborough. My second wife Patty was home.
My true love Mary, they say she is dead. This was our ring.'
John Clare unclenches his palm. The Gypsy reaches, lightly,
and pretends to marvel. 'It is a fine craftily matter, John.
Our blacksmiths would wonder. To smelt the purity
of air, and hammer it to something hidden yet lovely.
You must have loved her, friend, as if she was your own.'
Wisdom Smith glances: 'What do you want for the thing?'
'I want Mary to live so I can believe the world alive again'.
'Patty is your wife.' But Dead Mary watches the Gypsy.
She stares out from John to his friend of all friends.
Believe in me, she whispers as John Clare breathes: 'Believe me.'

The Strayed

'The world plays me like a kite, Wisdom; fame
like a gale hauls me high, firm on my frame –
sunshine on a harvest will do the same;
but one bleak word, or no word, and the strain
wrenches all my string.' 'You live by the smile
and frown of men. You bind yourself servile
to the sobbings of sparrows. Forgo them.'
John Clare watches his children play on the green.
'I cannot leave Northborough, my wives and home.'
'Their doors will always be on a latch, John,
however far you choose to stray from them.
Look. At me. How often have I upped and gone
yet you see me as though I never strayed?
The world will leave you, brother. I shall stay.'

Harebells

John Clare puts down his violin. 'Is there quickening wisdom
in the road and heath that sits hushed in a home and family?
– I mean the music of life moving. Swallows, swans, fieldfares.
These are ever nearer to me, more so because they never stay.'
Wisdom Smith tugs corks on two bottles. He pulls a long face.
'John, I know no man more half-in or half-out of your race.
You covet our roving – you are no bad scraper at the fiddle –
but you will never join us because you love' – gestures Wisdom –
'you love all this. We are like the harebells around us, brother:
everywhere and unseen; clear-eyed as those night-blue bells;
rebounding from the trudge and trample of night and day;
outstaring weather; blooming on into the first autumn gales.'
The dusk wind blows out the lamps of all the heath's flowers.
'We die if we do not move, whereas John – John, you would die.'

The Act

Wisdom swings to his feet as if pulled by an invisible hand.
'I shall show how this world wags without making one sound.'
And the Gypsy transforms himself first into a lawyer. He bends
a burning eye on invisible jurors. He simpers. He stands on his head
as the Judge and thunders silent sentence. Then Wisdom levitates
to tip-toe in pity and pride as a Reverend bent over his Bible
while an invisible scaffold gasps and bounces from a rope's recoil.
The Gypsy hangs kicking until hacked down by invisible blades.
The world grinds to a stop on invisible springs, bearings and axis.
'Do you ever tell lies, Wisdom?' 'All the long day through, brother,'
laughs the Gypsy. He lights his long pipe beneath his hat's brim.
'But the brassest of lies' – the Gypsy plucks – 'are like this heather:
a charm against visible harm and' – he crushes it – 'invisible harm.'
And the friends look at each other across the invisible stage of grass.

The Gypsy and the Poet

My house moves nowhere, hauled by invisible horses.
Shades shift around me, warming their hands at my hearth.
It has rained speech-marks down the windows' pages,
gathering a broken language in pools on their ledges
before letting it slither into the hollows of the earth.
My child stares out of windows on a pouring planet.
To him perhaps it is raining everywhere and forever.
I told myself this once. It is why I do not forget it;
although forty years have passed yet I am no older.
When Gypsy people speak aloud to one another
across greenway and hollow-way they say sister and brother.
When mother or father speak aloud to their children
they say our own daughter and they say our own son.
I call out to my child, and he is everywhere, and she is everyone.

'broken language': *Poggadi Jibb* or Romani

Epilogue

Spinning

But these two things shall come to thee
in a moment in one day, the loss of children,
and widowhood: they shall come upon thee
in their perfection for the multitude of thy sorceries
and for the great abundance of thine enchantments.
                                   – Isaiah 47

1

I love those stories when the world they wake
whitens on the horizon of your own eye
as though another sun has neared us in the night
or some new star flowered from the dark matter.
They shift on a single movement of mind or image –
a suicide leaps into space but lands on a high ledge
where he is found by fishermen with ropes and jokes.
The man says he thought the night was his own death
and it was, nearly. His hair has sprung into white fright
as if his head had been dipped into the dyes of the dawn.

What's expected of me, more so because unexpected,
is that I will go on telling and making and spinning,
more so because I was guilty of the crime called happiness.
Stories for children when we know all of us are children.
And now that I possess only my own poised possession
that I shall deliver these tales from some darker attention.
There they squat around the fires, with their teeth glittering.
They are moving on from their roll-ups to their shared pipes,
from red wine to glugs of gold whiskey. They are settling in
as if they were waiting for some long haul between settlements.

They say language shows you, so my stories should show you
what worlds I've wound through, whose voices I've breathed in –
that smoke spooling from their mouths, the fire's breath
swirling above them, make an understood utterance, a ghost
of what we see, what we pass through and what might be watching
us watching ourselves waiting. If that's too curdled for you
try truth. A five-year old boy dies. His parents bide by his body
for three days. Then they fill a rucksack with his best-loved toys.
Another rucksack embraces the child's body. They drive to a cliff,
hitch on the rucksacks and throw themselves spinning off the earth.

What does their tale say about how much they loved each other
and how much their son loved and was loved? Their story
makes something cease in you. They drove as if going on holiday
in a campervan. They say language shows you, and this story
shows to me that truth and even love grow impossibly possible.
This is not what you have come for. It is not what you wanted.
Where is the magic-eyed metaphor that reverses them into life?
Why am I not spilling word-lotions into your ears that allow
these three loving people to meet in another place, laughing
and singing and unbroken? Why doesn't the story wake the boy?

My own story interests nobody, not now I'm on my own.
Making story costs them nothing but my drink and caravan.
It's the hour before I begin when the clouds close down
and I'm lacking of language and in a desert of image
and nothing knows nothing. I am not even nowhere.
Now the word-trail slows in my mind, my blood sheds
all sugar and I can recognise no thing, not even the walls
of my van, or who I am, or what I will later, maybe, become.
I used to reach out at these times, touch my wife and say
'my wife'; then I would come back. I would come back into life.

2

The fire may as well be language for translating the logs
from their green, spitting blocks into red pictures and paintings.
The children spy wide worlds from the ringside of the fireside
as if a circus were performing before them. It shows in their eyes
for it is all reflected there. I usually start the evening with a call
to calm, then a joke and a drink before I unleash the creatures.
Animal tales first, padding around the fire just there in the dark,
now in the ring of light, and back again; I go out of sight
for the ending. Then stories about witches (the children dozing)
and so on to burkers and ghosts before night swallows my voice.

They say language shows you but subject shows you too.
Reverse that order of telling and you end up killing the evening,
sending the children unarmed into nightmare, startling
the rabbits of the audience with glare of monster and murder.
Yet one day, one day I shall never be there, not that I am now.
I stalk that ring of light. I know to toe around every twig.
I know when to lower my voice, and when to stop silent.
That's when I let natural magic have its effect—an owl call;
a dog fox wooing demonically in the wood; badgers scratching
and sputtering. These are not words; they are warier than words.

They are life not legend and sometimes they flout me.
They do not enter on cue. They make witty what is deadly
or horror from humour. Control. Do I really want control?
When their hearts are hearing me while their eyes are on the fire
it is as if I were the fire's brother, that we were a double act.
The fire came free (although children fed it until sleep).
Just pictures and paintings. We'd see them anyway in dreams.
What's expected of me is that I feed their dreams, lobbing
green blocks of words that spit and split and charm and char
while all the long, wordy night I am desperate to be doused.

What's fabulous might be a hedgehog spiny with rhyme
or a bride born from gnarled nouns. What's fabulous might be
darkness drowsing over a woman of words beside a waterfall
of words. What's fabulous might be an anvil hammered white-hot
with hurt, or Lipizzans held or hurtling on the harness of a verb.
Truth or tale, you've winnowed my mind many times too many
for me to be free with feigning, and now night's met my heart
and halved it. This is something I cannot say tonight, for tonight
is my last night. Tonight at midnight I am laying down my words.
I shall bury them beneath the embers of my brother, the fire.

I am sloughing the freight of fiction, the shackling story.
I owe this to my wife for believing in the one truth of me.
I am leaving the camp by dawn. I am taking nothing
apart from myself. The enchantment I offered as payment,
they will find it under fire. They will shovel it out ashen,
riven beyond repair. Stories are second chance. They repair.
They repay. I am broken. I want to try the truth. So,
I am glad you are all here. I hope you enjoy your evening.
I was here all the time listening to you but now it's my turn.
Ladies and gentlemen, and children. I am ready when you are ready.

Notes

Romani

The dialects that make up the Romani language offer an opening, not a fence, between fields of language. Romani contains so many words and phrases from other languages; language is absorbed as it is travelled through. The words are pronounced exactly as they appear, and their meaning is best caught by reading the poems aloud at a canter without leaning too hard into the glossary, and by listening to the meaning through the verbal music of the words. When a Romani word has two or more meanings in English, all those meanings are in play.

Poems

'Hedgehurst': my version drew inspiration from Duncan Williamson's version in *Fireside Tales* (1985) but is very much a free adaptation of the tale.

'Clearing a Name': *muck* is a term for family or clan; *Gaujo* is the term used by Roma for non-Romani. As with 'taig' (Catholic Irish) or 'gyp' (traveller) the terms are pejorative but used freely in Romani conversation.

'You Were Broken' opens on an image of an araucaria in a poem of the same title by Ungaretti.

'Sèsi o Lety U Písku': Nazi concentration camp for Roma from Bohemia, responsible for the eradication of more than half of the Roma population in the Czech lands.

'Ludus Coventriae': what we know as *Ludus Coventriae* is a collection of Mystery Plays that were once thought to have been presented in Coventry (the plays as such are not *of* Coventry). The *Coventry Carols*, however, are a series of songs from *The Pageant of the Shearmen and Taylors* and *The Pageant of the Weavers*. Members of those guilds and also perhaps professional players performed these 'true' Coventry Corpus Christi plays in Coventry during the celebrations on Corpus Christi Day, the religious festival closest to Midsummer. The carols within the plays have entered folk memory as lullabies. 'Ludus Coventriae' borrows phrases from these plays and excerpts from the carols. 'The Charges on Midsummer Night' is freely adapted from *Records of Early English Drama: Coventry*, edited by R.W. Ingram.

'Kings': the *Book of the Wisdom of the Egyptians* deals in field-knowledge of the Romani. It is a kind of hedgerow schoolbook for travelling people. It contains sayings for survival, for living on edges, including within the margins of error imposed by the demands and prejudices of Gajo (non-gypsies) should offence be taken, and the law, or worse, be thrown against a travelling group or tribe My language sources for this poem include the website on Romani culture, the Patrin Web Journal (http://www.geocities. com/Paris/5121/patrin.htm) and its Romanichal Word List. I have also used *The Gypsy–English English–Gypsy Concise Dictionary* by Atanas Slavov (New York, 1999). Two phrases, including the epigraph to 'Kings', are adapted from *Romano Lavo-Lil* by George Burrow, 1974 edition. The phrase 'little wicked wicket gate' comes from Edwin Muir's 'The Castle'. Atanas Slavov writes in *The Gypsy–English English–Gypsy Concise Dictionary*: 'Word stress does not play a significant role in the Gypsy language. It is presented in this work the way words were pronounced by the Gypsies we inter-viewed. If the interviewees or the written sources we used show differences in applying stresses in certain words, we do not show them'. à, è, ì, ò, ù, òo – stressed vowels.

'Taken Away': a free adaptation of a well-known traveller and folk tale. 'The Taen-Awa' in Duncan Williamson's *The King and the Lamp: Scottish Traveller Tales* (Canongate, 2000) provided my way into writing the poem.

'The Circling Game': the narrative took inspiration from the rendition of this traveller's tale in 'The Boy and the Blacksmith' from Duncan Williamson's *The King and the Lamp: Scottish Traveller Tales* (Canongate, 2000).

'The Library Beneath the Harp': the poet Bronisława Wajs (1908–87) was known by her Romani name Papusza which means 'doll'. She grew up on the road in Poland within her kumpania or band of families. She was literate and learned to read and write by trading food for lessons. Her reading and writing were frowned upon and whenever she was found reading she was beaten and the book destroyed. She was married at fifteen to a much older and revered harpist, Dionýzy Wajs. Unhappy in marriage, she took to singing as an outlet for her frustrations, with her husband often accompanying her on harp. She then began to compose her own poems and songs. When the Second World War broke out, and Roma were being murdered in Poland by both the German Nazis and the Ukrainian fascists, they gave up their carts and horses but not their harps. With heavy harps on their backs, they looked for hiding places in the woods. 35,000 Roma out of 50,000 were murdered during the war in Poland. The Wajs clan hid in the forest in Volyň, hungry, cold and terrified. A horrible experience inspired Papusza to write her longest poem, 'Ratfale jasfa – so pal sasendyr pšegijam upre Volyň 43 a 44 berša' ('Bloody tears – what we endured from German soldiers in Volyň in '43 and '44'), parts of which are used in 'The Library Beneath the Harp'. In 1949 Papusza was heard by the Polish poet Jerzy Ficowski, who recognised her talent. Ficowski published several of her poems in a magazine called *Problemy* along with an anti-nomadic interview with Polish poet Julian Tuwim. Ficowski became an adviser on 'the Gypsy Question', and used Papusza's poems to make his case against nomadism. This led to the forced settlement of the Roma all over Poland in 1950, known variously as 'Action C' or 'the Great Halt'. The Roma community began to regard Papusza as a traitor, threatening her and calling her names. Papusza maintained that Ficowski had exploited her work and had taken it out of context. Her appeals were ignored and the Baro Shero (Big Head, an elder in the Roma community) declared her 'unclean'. She was banished from the Roma world, and even

Ficowski broke contact with her. Afterwards, she spent eight months in a mental asylum and then the next thirty-four years of her life alone and isolated. Her tribe laid a curse on Papusza's poems and upon anybody using or performing her work. 'The Library Beneath the Harp' partly borrows and reshapes some of Papusza's introductory autobiography from the *Songs of Papusza* as well as three of her poems.

'A Lit Circle': the epigraph is from *Josser: The Secret Life of a Circus Girl* (Virago, 2000) by Nell Stroud, now Nell Gifford, owner of Gifford's Circus.

Index of Titles

Index of First Lines